I sent messengers to them, saying, "I am doing a great work, so that I cannot come down. Why should the work cease . . . ?"

(NEHEMIAH 6:3)

Rebuild

Rebuild
Restoring Your God-Given Identity

Copyright © 2022 by Marilyn Hickey Ministries

All rights reserved. No part of this book may be reproduced or transmitted in any form or by any means, electronic or mechanical, including photocopying, recording, or by any information storage and retrieval system, without permission in writing from the publisher.

Marilyn Hickey Ministries
P.O. Box 6598
Englewood, CO 80155
marilynandsarah.org

Edited by Bobbie Sartini, Nancy Buckner, and Sarah Heaton

ISBN 978-1-938696-29-9

Scripture quotations marked KJV are taken from the King James Version®. Public domain.

Unless otherwise indicated, all Scripture quotations are taken from the New King James Version®. Copyright © 1982 by Thomas Nelson. Used by permission. All rights reserved.

Scripture quotations marked NRSV are taken from the New Revised Standard Version Bible, copyright © 1989 National Council of the Churches of Christ in the United States of America. Used by permission. All rights reserved worldwide.

Scripture quotations marked ESV are taken from the ESV® Bible (The Holy Bible, English Standard Version®), copyright © 2001 by Crossway, a publishing ministry of Good News Publishers. Used by permission. All rights reserved.

Scripture quotations marked NASB are taken from the (NASB®) New American Standard Bible®, Copyright © 1960, 1971, 1977, 1995, 2020 by The Lockman Foundation. Used by permission. All rights reserved. http://www.lockman.org

Printed in the United States of America.

Assembled and Produced for Marilyn Hickey Ministries by
Breakfast for Seven
2150 E. Continental Blvd., Southlake, TX 76092
breakfastforseven.com

Marilyn Hickey

Rebuild

Restoring Your God-Given Identity

Marilyn & Sarah
MARILYN HICKEY MINISTRIES

Contents

Introduction ix

Chapter One
Rebuilding the Wall 1

Chapter Two
The Gates of Authority in Your Identity — Part One 31

Chapter Three
The Gates of Authority in Your Identity — Part Two 55

Chapter Four
Overcoming the Enemy of Your Identity 75

Chapter Five
God's Remedy for an Inferiority Complex 97

Chapter Six
Dedicating Your Identity to God 117

Chapter Seven
God Can Stabilize an Unstable Identity 131

Chapter Eight
Identity Change Brings Appetite for the Word.................................. 149

Chapter Nine
Resurrection Bread to Feed Your Identity... 159

Chapter Ten
Your Identity Can Draw Interest 175

Chapter Eleven
Two Confessions for a Balanced Identity 191

Chapter Twelve
Our Identities Are Important to God 213

Chapter Thirteen
A New You.. 231

End Notes.. 243

Receive Jesus Christ as Lord and Savior of Your Life 247

About Marilyn Hickey... 251

To learn more about Marilyn Hickey Ministries............................... 255

Introduction

The subject of identity has become a hot-button issue in the last several years. Self-help books and blogs abound, and more and more people are consulting mental health experts to find out "who they really are." They delve into the past, looking for clues to their identities, searching genealogy websites to learn where they came from. There's nothing wrong with wanting to know your family's history. However, even more important than understanding where you came from is realizing who God made you to be and that He made you in His image (Genesis 1:26).

When you were born, you had a destiny, a divine appointment, already planned for you from before the foundation of the world. As a born-again Christian, you are uniquely created to fulfill a specific purpose and you have a unique calling that only *you* can fulfill.

God wants you to fulfill every facet of your identity and accomplish all you set your hand to, just as He does. Romans 8:29 echoes this: *"For whom He foreknew, He also predestined to be conformed to the image of His Son, that He might be the firstborn among many brethren."* The way to fulfill your place in His kingdom is to conform to the identity of Jesus Christ.

Many people mistakenly try to imitate someone else's image, ministry, or calling. It's fine to admire other people — but it's wrong to assume that your ministry call is the same as someone else's. Each of us needs to discover our personal identity and purpose in Christ. Second Corinthians 3:18 tells us how this is done: *"We all, with unveiled face, beholding as in a mirror the glory of the Lord, are being transformed into the same image from glory to glory, just as by the Spirit of the Lord."*

Unfortunately, many Christians are discontented because they have taken their eyes off the identity that God has for them. They start looking at their circumstances or other Christians to compare themselves — but that's not what God has called us to

Introduction

focus on! God is the only one who can complete or "repair" your identity.

Romans 12:2 tells you how to walk in God's image: *"Do not be conformed to this world, but be transformed by the renewing of your mind, that you may prove what is that good and acceptable and perfect will of God."* The Word of God is the mirror of all that He has for you — when you look in it and see Him, you recognize your image. When you behold Him and fulfill His image for you, God's perfect plan for your life will go from glory to glory!

Identity Theft

We are three-fold beings, created in the image of God. God wants us to be whole — spirit, soul, and body. Notice that spirit comes first. That's important to know because so many times as Christians, we don't see the identity we have in the spirit. We try to identify our relationship with God through the soul.

Since our souls are comprised of our minds, emotions, and wills, we may try to hear through our minds. Or we want to feel through our emotions. "If this is God, I need to feel it is true," we tell ourselves. Or we try to do things through willpower alone. "I'm not going to smoke anymore. I'm not going to drink anymore. I'm not going to lose my temper anymore. I'm not going to spend money foolishly anymore." And on and on we go. Or we think of our physical body with all five senses. Sometimes we try to get to God through our senses. "Well, if I could see Him, hear an audible voice, or touch Him, then I would know it was God speaking to me."

Before the fall, all of that was possible. Adam and Eve were able to talk with God and walk with Him. God communicated directly with them because He had put His spirit in them. Their beings — spirits, souls, and bodies — the whole of their identities were intrinsically tied to God. They were brilliant! Adam named all the animals and could remember their names. Many of us are doing well to remember somebody's name five minutes after being introduced to them! They had a job to do as well. Adam and Eve were in charge of the garden and had dominion over the earth.

But the devil knew that if he could get them to fall into sin, then they would no longer be connected with God. They would be disconnected from God in their spirits. He plotted their downfall — and ours — through his number-one tool, deception. He came to Eve, deceiving her into believing his lie that God was trying to keep something good from them — that they would be as wise as God. What a crock! They were already walking in godly wisdom because they were one in spirit with God. But you know what Eve did. She ate the fruit. She got Adam to eat as well, and they fell. They lost their connection through the spirit as a result. Satan stole their identities.

> **When you blow it — when you say the wrong things or do the wrong things — the devil likes to make you doubt God's forgiveness.**

So now, in a fallen world, how do we connect with and reach God? Our senses don't tell us who we are or who God created us to be. The key is the spirit. We connect with God through our spirits, and we identify with Him through our spirits. Remember, *"God is Spirit, and those who worship Him must worship in spirit and truth"* (John 4:24).

Satan knows this. He would love to help you forget that you are made like God and loved by God. When you blow it — when you say the wrong things or do the wrong things — the devil likes to make you doubt God's forgiveness. He likes to say, "Well, you've just screwed up too many times. God doesn't love you anymore."

John 10:10 says, *"The thief [Satan] does not come except to steal, and to kill, and to destroy . . ."* The number-one thing the devil wants to do to you is steal, kill, and destroy your identity. And is he ever bold. He even tried to steal Jesus's identity! It's the first thing he tried to do with Jesus at the beginning of His earthly ministry.

> **. . . through Jesus you can become the whole person God created you to be.**

In Matthew chapter three, when Jesus was baptized, God says, *"This is My beloved Son, in whom I am well pleased"* (v. 17). After His baptism, Jesus was led by the Spirit into the wilderness to be tempted by the devil. Satan tempted Him repeatedly, saying, *"If you are the Son of God . . ."* (Matthew 4:3, 6). It is here that

Introduction

Satan tried to challenge Jesus's identity. However, God didn't just say, "This is my Son." God said, "This is my *beloved* Son." Jesus knew who He was, who His Father was, what His calling was, and what Satan was trying to do. Unlike Eve, He wasn't deceived. He defeated Satan by answering with the Word of God: "*It is written*" (Matthew 4:4, 7, 10). You can defeat the devil in the same way.

In the second part of John 10:10, Jesus says, "*I have come that* [you] *may have life, and that* [you] *may have it more abundantly.*" Jesus came to give us victory! Through His finished work on the cross, we become born-again, made new, and in the image of Christ. No matter what kind of walls you may have built around yourself or allowed the devil to build around you, no matter what you have done in the past, or who you were before Christ came into your life, through Jesus you can become the whole person God created you to be. You are now the temple of the Holy Spirit (1 Corinthians 6:19-20). Let's start rebuilding the walls of that temple the devil has destroyed.

Chapter One

Rebuilding the Wall

:::

In Colossians 3:10, Paul tells us to *"Put on the new man who is renewed in knowledge according to the image of Him who created him."* The Greek word used for "renewed" in this passage is *anakainóō* which also means to "renovate."

According to Proverbs 25:28, *"Whoever has no rule over his own spirit is like a city broken down, without walls."* In other words, a person who fails to control his identity is subject to attack because he is disconnected from God. When the walls of a city are down, that is when the enemy can come and conquer that city. Likewise, when the walls of our temples are down, the enemy can come and steal our identities from us. That brings great grief to God. Those whom

He made in His image and gave His Spirit are disconnected, as if their spirits are dead to Him when He desires to speak to them. It grieved Him so much that He set in motion a plan to reconnect mankind to Him again so we could have a spiritual relationship with Him. Our goal is to get the walls of our identities rebuilt so that we can be fit temples in which God can dwell.

Rebuilding a People's Identity

I found the most beautiful typology of how to rebuild damaged areas of our identities in the Old Testament book of Nehemiah.

If you look into the historical background, you will find that the Israelites started out as a group of murmuring and complaining people who became discontented, especially when they took their eyes off the identity that God had earmarked for them. They started looking at circumstances or the images and identities of other people around them — and that was not what God had called them to focus on! Circumstances and people will change, but God never changes. He is the only one who can complete your identity. God had called Israel to be a people set apart from the heathen nations of the world to worship the one true God who would one day send the Savior of the world through this nation. But they went after the world instead, forsaking God's chosen identity for them as a nation. As a result, they went into captivity. The Israelites lived in captivity for 70 years because of idolatry. They lost their identity as a nation and instead became subjects of the ungodly, idol-worshiping kings of Assyria, Babylon, and Persia. It was a terrible time when they pined away for their God. After 70 years of captivity, which had been prophesied by Jeremiah, God told Israel, "Your time of punishment is over. You have been cleansed from idolatry, so I am going to let you return to rebuild my temple." Not only that, the Jews who returned from captivity had the burden of rebuilding their own identities and their national identity while still subject to foreign powers.

The book of Ezra tells of how over 49,000 Israelites returned to Israel following their captivity (538–516 B.C.) and, under the direction of Zerubbabel, rebuilt the temple (Ezra 1:1–4). Some 57 years after the temple was rebuilt, Ezra, a priest and scribe, was sent by God back to Jerusalem with a burden to teach the Law and reestablish the covenant. Nehemiah was sent under the royal authority of King Artaxerxes to Jerusalem from 458 B.C. to 420 B.C. (he made a couple of trips back and forth). Ezra and Nehemiah were contemporaries.

When the Israelites returned from exile to Jerusalem, they rebuilt God's temple. When Jesus enters our hearts and lives within us, the Bible tells us that we become temples of God: *"Do you not know that you are the temple of God and that the Spirit of God dwells in you?"* (1 Corinthians 3:16). When the Holy Spirit comes to dwell in our hearts by faith, God looks around and says, "This temple needs the protection of walls to keep the enemy out."

The Holy Spirit is the Master Rebuilder

The book of Nehemiah chronicles the building of the walls surrounding the city of Jerusalem after the temple was rebuilt. In this book, Nehemiah is sent by God to help make the temple safe from enemy onslaughts against Israel. The heart's desire of Nehemiah was to see the temple safe again. Because the walls had been broken down, the gates had crumbled. God put a tremendous burden on Nehemiah to mend the situation.

God paid an expensive price to purchase these things for us; and if He bought us, He won't let us sit there like pieces of junk!

It is interesting that the meaning of Nehemiah's name is "consolation of Jehovah." In Luke 2:25, we are told that Simeon, a devout man, was waiting for the consolation of Israel — Jesus. In Greek, "consolation" is *paraklēsis* and means "comforter, consoler." Just as Nehemiah brought comfort to his people through the rebuilding and the promise of safety, the Holy Spirit is our comforter who wants to rebuild our identities. When He enters our hearts, He examines our identities and begins a new process of restoration. The Comforter has come to strengthen our hearts and says, "I want to make you like Jesus."

You ask, "Does He really enjoy restoring my identity?" I know that He does, and I saw this in Matthew 18, a beautiful picture of a shepherd who made a great effort to restore one lost sheep to his large sheepfold.

A shepherd had a flock of 100 sheep, one of which wandered into the wilderness. Finding a sheep missing, the shepherd left his other 99 sheep in search of the one. The shepherd had to go to the mountains, climbing over rocks, hills, and brambles, and perhaps even falling several times. He probably crossed streambeds and who knows what else. But when he finally found the lamb, his task had only begun. He had to return home, carrying the sheep on his shoulders with its legs tied around his neck.

Did the shepherd consider the restoration of one sheep to the fold to be a drag and a drain? No way. In fact, the Bible says that he rejoiced, and when he brought the lamb home, all the neighbors probably rejoiced, too. God rejoices in restoring your identity.

You will find that Nehemiah was a "type" of the Holy Spirit, and his complete strength and attention was focused on restoring Jerusalem's walls. Why was he so concerned about the walls of Jerusalem? The answer is found in the very first chapter:

> *"But if you return to Me, and keep My commandments and do them, though some of you were cast out to the farthest part of the heavens, yet I will gather them from there, and bring them to the place which I have chosen as a dwelling for My name."*
> (NEHEMIAH 1:9)

God says, "Do you see this born-again Christian? I have set my name on him. He is a Christian now, and I love him because he bears my Son's name. Since that person bears my name, I don't want him to have a nasty disposition. I don't want him biting other people's heads off and being ugly. I want him to be like me." Then Nehemiah 1:10 tells you another reason that God wants to restore our identities: *"Now these are Your servants and Your people, whom You have redeemed by Your great power, and by Your strong hand."*

The word "redeemed" means "to buy back." We sing hymns about being "redeemed by the blood of the Lamb," yet do we know what those words mean? We have been bought by God with the most expensive possession He owned: the blood of His only Son,

Jesus Christ. "To buy back" says so much. When God bought us, we were set free to do His will, freed from physical disease, and taken from prison and bondage into freedom. God paid an expensive price to purchase these things for us; and if He bought us, He won't let us sit there like pieces of junk! He is going to restore us by conforming our identities to His Son's perfect image.

In the second chapter, you see Nehemiah venturing toward Jerusalem. As soon as he arrives there, the enemy comes out — angry, upset, and ready for violence. One of the first things that happens to us when Jesus begins revealing some areas for restoration in our lives is that the enemy says, "Uh-oh." You can even see his thoughts:

> *When Sanballat the Horonite and Tobiah the Ammonite official heard of it, they were deeply disturbed that a man had come to seek the well-being of the children of Israel.*
> **(NEHEMIAH 2:10)**

As we previously touched on, it grieves the devil when he sees the Holy Spirit enter your life for the purpose of enhancing your well-being and bringing you life at its best. It upsets the devil, and you can especially see this when you know one of the meanings of "Sanballat" is "enemy in secret."

Both God and the devil have a plan for your identity. God's plans for you are good; the devil's plans are for destruction. What components make up your identity? Remember, we said earlier that we are spirit, soul, and body. All of these work in tandem to form our identity. When you are saved, your spirit is in communion and communication with the Spirit of God. This connection is generally unseen by others. What others see, however, are the soul and body. This is where you think, feel, and choose.

Nursing the Hurts of the Past

The walls of Jerusalem in the book of Nehemiah are similar to the walls that make up your identity. With the rebuilding of the wall, the people began to rebuild their own identities as well. The return of the exiles hadn't gone well so far. They thought this would be the fulfillment of Ezekiel's prophecy of the dry bones coming to life (see Ezekiel 37:1–14). Instead, they were confronted with one crisis after another, and their hopes for the restoration of their nation were fizzling out due to great opposition. Like the Hebrews who left Egypt before them, who had to get the identity of "slave" out of their thinking, they had to get the identity of "captive" out of their thinking and rebuild their own individual identities in order to restore their identity as a nation:

> *"Here we are, slaves to this day — slaves in the land that you gave to our ancestors to enjoy its fruit and its good gifts. Its rich yield goes to the kings whom you have set over us because of our sins; they have power also over our bodies and over our livestock at their pleasure, and we are in great distress."*
> (NEHEMIAH 9:36-37 NRSV)

The gates are even more specific: they are the places of authority where you make decisions. God is very concerned about the choices you make in your life. He wants to lead you to make decisions by the direction of His Spirit. God is your ultimate authority.

To accomplish this, God has provided you with three main gifts to enhance your identity. In your thinking, He has given you the mind of Christ. In your emotions, He has given you the ability to react supernaturally; and in your decisions, He has given you spiritual leading by the Holy Spirit.

In addition, when you were saved, another miracle took place: "[God] *has delivered us from the power of darkness and conveyed us into the kingdom of the Son of His love"* (Colossians 1:13). Not only were your sins forgiven, but you also became a new creation with a new nature. You're not in darkness anymore. Now you have dominion, and your identity is established in Christ's. Satan no longer has any authority over your identity — unless you open the gate to him in some area of your life. You are meant to always triumph in Christ. You are supposed to win!

Thankfully, God sent Nehemiah and Ezra to help correct the thinking of the exiles, rebuild their identities, and heal the wounds of their captivity by rebuilding their self-confidence. They rebuilt the walls and repaired and rehung the gates of their beloved Jerusalem, that had fallen down.

Using the Bricks of Our Pasts

Nehemiah wanted to build a strong wall, but when he came to Jerusalem, there was quite a task ahead. The walls lay in piles of rubble. Nehemiah had been in Jerusalem for three days; while the town slept, on the third day, he arose to have a closer look at the damage. Three is the number of resurrection. Nehemiah wanted to see what would be involved in resurrecting the ruins of Jerusalem's walls and gates.

God is so economical; He takes your old, useless past life and uses it to create a productive present.

Looking over the scene, Nehemiah saw rubble, rubble, rubble. There were broken and burned bricks, and debris lay everywhere. Despair and anguish must have filled him. However, he was on a mission from God, and hope produces vision. I think, *The Holy Spirit wants to take the rubbish and debris from our past lives and sweep it away forever.*

"Bad" walls can also come down and/or be repaired. The people of East Germany truly rejoiced

Rebuilding the Wall

on November 9, 1989, when the Berlin Wall was opened following years of communist oppression. The rubbish and debris were swept away forever, and now they have rebuilt a new life in a reunited Germany. They have built a new identity for themselves. Ironically, the site of the Berlin wall is now a tourist attraction.

Studying the book of Nehemiah, I discovered that it is not the Holy Spirit's plan to sweep away the broken bricks. His plan is to *rebuild* the walls, not build brand new ones. God is so economical; He takes your old, useless past life and uses it to create a productive present.

Through the years as a pastor's wife and in my ministry, I have been amazed to watch how God will save a young drug addict, fill him with the Spirit, deliver him from his addiction, and then send him right back to minister where he came from. The young person becomes a witness and an instrument to win former friends to Christ. His past becomes a strengthening force to help win people with similar pasts.

God can make your past a blessing, too. In Nehemiah, the old debris was actually useful! Likewise, the Holy Spirit will use your past experience and turn it into something that glorifies God.

After seeing the rubble surrounding the walls of Jerusalem and the city gates gone or destroyed, Nehemiah said to himself, *This must all be restored to its original condition.* But Nehemiah was not planning to do the job alone; he would have the help of the whole city!

Rebuilding Is Not a One-Person Job

Following his nighttime inspection of the walls, I'm sure Nehemiah heard the Holy Spirit giving him that directive. Most of the time, it's a still, small voice, and you have to get still to hear it. When you hear His voice, it's usually an impression that comes to you saying something like, "I want you to do X, Y, and Z" or, as in Nehemiah's case, "Go to Jerusalem and rebuild the walls."

The Holy Spirit is not going to build your identity all by Himself. Of course, like Nehemiah, He directs the work that takes place. But just as Nehemiah called on the people of Jerusalem for help, the Holy Spirit will use other people in your life. That is His plan:

Then I said to them, "You see the distress that we are in, how Jerusalem lies waste, and its gates are burned with fire. Come and let us build the wall of Jerusalem, that we may no longer be a reproach." (NEHEMIAH 2:17)

Nehemiah said, "We are *all* involved in this project. Let *us* build." The Holy Spirit is present to direct the work in your soul and use your past, but He will also use people to help. God will place all kinds of personalities in your life to rebuild the walls and gates, and when I say, "all kinds," I mean it! Sometimes He will use someone unexpected because that person was the only one who could take care of a certain area of your life.

Studying all the gates in Nehemiah (and you will see them in more detail later), you find that all kinds of people helped rebuild the walls and hang the gates. There were goldsmiths, pharmacists, daughters, noblemen, and Gibeonites. God does not say, "I'll just send really neat people with whom you have a great deal in common." He may send people you don't even like! He may even use unsaved people to help you.

It is very dangerous for us to close doors to certain people because "they aren't our type." I have been guilty of it. I have said, "God, we don't see eye-to-eye on things." God replied, "Don't close that door. I have sent that person to you to be of use in your life."

Some years ago, a woman in our church was really troublesome. She was very caustic and critical. Our church was called "Happy Church," so we should be happy, right? But that woman was bad advertising for us!

Once a year we held a business meeting, and one year when she attended the meeting, it wasn't a happy one. This woman stood up and said some really nasty things. She acted as though my husband and I were thugs, and she asked questions insinuating, "What are you *really* doing? Do the people *really* know what is happening?"

Her words cut me deeply. I must be honest that my attitude was very unspiritual. As the woman spoke, I turned around and gave a look that said, "Why don't you sit down and shut up?" Of course, she didn't look at me at all. She just went on asking questions.

The only person really damaged by that meeting was me. The rest of those present for the meeting knew the woman's attitudes were less than spiritual, so they ignored her actions. But on the way home, my husband said, "Wasn't that a good business meeting?" I answered, "No, I thought it was terrible." He said, "You mean so-and-so? Oh, Marilyn, she is nothing to worry about." But the more I thought about the woman, the angrier I became. Soon, I had become bitter.

The business meeting had been on a Wednesday night. The following Sunday morning, as I greeted people after a church service, this woman raced over to me, grabbed and hugged me, and said, "Oh, I love you, sister."

I thought, *If that's love, forget it!* To be honest, I did not love her back at all. I didn't want her to tell me that she loved me, and I didn't say, "I love you, too." Instead, I just kind of mumbled, "God bless you."

That day, I went home with an ugly feeling inside toward that woman and did not realize that she would be used by God to rebuild a part of my identity that I desperately needed. Out of this experience, I would receive a revelation from God that I had never seen.

During the day on Sunday, I thought, *We are having Communion tonight.* The Bible says that you can drink judgment to yourself if you take Communion when you have fought against your brother. I thought, *I don't want to drink judgment to myself.* I began to pray and pray, *Oh, God, help me forgive her.* The more I prayed, the less forgiving I felt! I became more and more upset with the woman.

For Communion, we dimmed the lights and quietly sang and worshiped the Lord. Then people came and took Communion as they felt spiritually prepared. Voluntarily, people would come to the altar, kneel, and be served Communion.

I thought, *I cannot take Communion with this terrible unforgiveness. Nobody will know it anyway because the lights will be down.* The only person who might have known would have been my husband, Wally, because we usually took Communion together. On the way to the church, I told him, "I won't be taking Communion tonight."

He almost fell out of the car!

He asked me why I wouldn't be taking Communion, and I explained, "I have unforgiveness in my heart." He said, "Oh, I just can't believe that." I thought his words were one of the sweetest compliments I'd ever received. He thought I couldn't feel unforgiving! I insisted, "It's true. I have unforgiveness, and I can't get rid of it." Wally asked me to pray with him, and afterward he said, "Well, do you feel better?"

"No, I feel worse."

We arrived at the church, held the service, and afterwards the lights were turned low for Communion to begin. I sat alone, in a negative frame of mind, and then I found out that God is a tattletale. No one would have known that I had missed Communion. But a woman from all the way across the church walked over to me and sat down. She said, "Marilyn, I feel led to take Communion with you tonight."

God had placed a brick in the wall of my identity about how to walk in forgiveness.

I thought, *God, why did you do that?* Then I told the woman, "I won't be taking Communion." She was almost as shocked as my husband had been! When she learned why, she nodded and said, "That's why the Lord sent me over here." She sat quietly for a few moments and then broke the silence, "Marilyn, you always tell us to take things by faith. Why can't you take forgiveness by faith?" When she said those words, it seemed that a light switched on and shone this Scripture into my spirit:

> *Anyone whom you forgive, I also forgive. Indeed, what I have forgiven, if I have forgiven anything, has been for your sake in the presence of Christ.* (2 CORINTHIANS 2:10 ESV)

I had been trying, trying, trying to forgive a sister all by myself. But I had not been forgiving her in the person of Jesus Christ. At that moment, I prayed, *Oh, Jesus, I forgive her. I take forgiveness by faith and forgive her with your ability, not my own.* That prayer set my spirit free to worship. I took Communion that night, and I will never forget that service. God had placed a brick in the wall of my identity about how to walk in forgiveness.

There is a sequel to this story. I never talked to the woman about my feelings toward her; but a month after the business meeting, she called and said, "I know that you are very busy with services. Tell me how I can come over to your house and leave a meal in your refrigerator."

What happened? After that, she called many more times and was always doing something sweet for my family. One day, as I prayed, the Lord said, "When you loosed forgiveness in heaven, you loosed it on earth. You loosed that woman to do good works. But until you forgave her, heaven was bound from moving on earth to release her. The love you feel for that woman came through your forgiveness."

Then the Lord reminded me, "Remember the stoning of Stephen? He prayed, *'Lord, do not charge them with this sin'* " (Acts 7:60). Stephen forgave Saul, who consented to the martyr's stoning. Later on, Saul was loosed to become Paul, one of Christ's apostles and a writer of the New Testament. When Stephen loosed forgiveness for Saul, heaven came to earth in his life.

On his way to Damascus, Saul fell to the ground under God's power, which came in a flash of blinding light. Saul cried out, "Lord? Who are you?" The Lord called him into ministry right then. Sometimes I think that God may have said, "Stephen didn't get to finish his work because you consented to his death. Now you get to finish it for him."

Can you see how God is using identities to rebuild the walls and gates of our lives? When we close doors to people we dislike, or people who are different, or people who are impossible to get along with, we may be closing the gates to someone whom the Holy Spirit has placed in our lives. God has a way for us to deal with those whom He sends to us, and we must not close our doors to them.

However, keep in mind that some people are not picked by God to help in a work. Some, as we shall see later, want to "help" when in reality they really want to thwart the work of the Lord. That's when it becomes imperative to fully listen for the still, small voice of the Spirit.

Getting Ready to Rebuild

We say that some people are extroverts because they open all the gates of their identity to let everyone in. Others we call introverts because the gates of their identity seem completely closed. Actually, both of these types of personalities need to be balanced as to how they deal with the people whom God sends. God wants us to know when to close the gates of our identity and when to open them. We are to have Spirit-led identities that are being restored to the image of Jesus.

Would you say that the walls of your identity have been broken in certain areas? The Holy Spirit wants, right now, to begin rebuilding the walls and gates of your identity.

You may say, "Oh, my past is terrible." But I looked at what God used to rebuild Jerusalem's walls, and He used burned bricks. Burned stones. It seemed very strange that He used burned materials, but then I began to see something special about them.

Today, when you go to buy stones or bricks for a building, the most expensive ones you can buy are those that have been used. The burned bricks make the most beautiful walls and fireplaces because they show contrast in their appearance. None are alike. God uses your past because there are certain people whom only you can reach.

You are a new creature in Christ Jesus. You are totally different from the person you were before being saved. People say, "I knew you before — but you have certainly changed!" They see the contrast that Jesus has made in your life, and it is beautiful.

Rebuild: Restoring Your God-Given Identity

Then God uses that contrast as a witness and to help you rebuild the walls of other people's identities. This change was so obvious in a friend of mine. He was into prostitution and bootlegging. His whole family were crooks and thugs. He used to take liquor across state lines and did some really raunchy things. He ended up in jail, where someone came and preached to him. He received Jesus as his Savior. His friends and family couldn't believe the change in him. He was so changed that he started a church in Louisville and went on to plant about 60 or 70 more churches. His son pastored that first church, and they started a TV station that reached across the whole world. How did that happen? He became a new creation and regained the identity God had planned for him!

The same is true for you. Whatever you may have been involved in in the past is now under the blood of Christ. You are a new creation in Christ. Old things have passed away and all things have become new. (see 2 Corinthians 5:17.)

We must be very keen to the Spirit's voice in helping other people. Sometimes I see older Christians approach new Christians and try to rebuild their walls without the Holy Spirit's help. The older, experienced Christian will say, "Stop smoking! You can't do this, and you can't do that!" But the younger believer does not accept the correction because there is no relationship and no bond in the Spirit yet.

The Wall

When Nehemiah went out alone at night to examine the city's walls, he was very much in tune with the voice of God. He stopped first by a place called the "Valley Gate," which led to the Valley of Hinnom which is a reference to hell. Nehemiah then made his way to the "Refuse Gate," which was nearby. This gate also led to the Valley of Hinnom, where the city's garbage was burned.

Near the Refuse Gate was a well called *"the Serpent Well"* (Nehemiah 2:13). Satan first appears in the Bible in the form of a serpent who tempted Eve into disobeying God's commands, allowing sin to enter the world. The judgment of sin is eternity in hell, but since Jesus took our judgment on the cross, Satan can no longer drag us into hell.

Around the well, there was a great deal of garbage and refuse. But Nehemiah didn't just rush in and start throwing everything away; he was waiting for the Lord to tell him his next move. In the same way, when we see garbage and trash in someone's life, particularly that of a young believer, we must be led by the Spirit in helping them. Otherwise, we could cause more harm than good.

I wondered why there was a pool by the gate, and I found that there was either a fountain, pool, spring, or well by every gate in the wall. Why would there be water? The water was there to put out the enemy's fiery darts!

The gates of your identity are where you make decisions. The Holy Spirit may say, "Close the gate, here comes the enemy." But when you close the gate, the enemy may throw a fiery dart to catch the gate on fire. That's when you use water to put out the fire and keep your fortress intact.

The water represents the washing of the water by God's Word. How did Jesus put out fiery darts from the enemy? Jesus said, "It is written," and then spoke God's Word. You have to have the Word, as well as the Spirit, if your identity is going to reflect God's best for you.

How wonderful it is for us to experience the benefit of having an identity like that of Jesus! It's exciting to know that God wants to restore our identities, day by day, in the power of the Holy Spirit. A transformed identity is God's high goal for us according to Philippians 2:13, *"For it is God who works in you both to will and to do for His good pleasure."* Remember, too, that Romans 8:37 says you are more than a conqueror through Christ, and you can do all things through Christ who strengthens you (Philippians 4:13). That's how a former pimp and bootlegger could become a pastor and church planter. His identity changed by becoming a new creation in Christ.

Grafting and Pruning

The Israelites didn't have to start from scratch when they started rebuilding. They already had much of the building materials they needed because it lay in rubble around them. They had to clean off the debris left behind from the destruction of the wall and use it to repair the existing foundation; then, by placing one brick upon another, they were able to rebuild the wall.

As a new creation, you have been grafted into Christ (John 15:2) and grafted in alongside God's people Israel (Romans 11:11–36). And God will continue to prune you to correspond to His design for you. Jesus is the vine, and we are the branches. Let's look at that process a little bit more.

Grafting requires wounding. The tree surgeon makes a cut in the host tree and must ensure that he accesses the nutrients in that tree, too. Then he cuts off a branch from another tree to graft into the host tree and sticks the cut-off branch into the cut made in the host tree so that it becomes one with the host tree. He then wraps a cloth around it and leaves it on until a new limb grows in and becomes a part of the host tree.

Notice, there's no grafting, unless there's a wounding. This tree had to be cut in order to graft another branch in. Jesus knew that He would have to be wounded for us to be grafted into His body.

> *He was wounded for our transgressions,*
> *He was bruised for our iniquities;*
> *The chastisement for our peace was upon Him,*
> *And by His stripes we are healed.* (ISAIAH 53:5)

Grafting comes through wounding. *"Therefore lay aside all filthiness and overflow of wickedness, and receive with meekness the implanted word, which is able to save your souls"* (James 1:21). That "implanting" has to do with grafting. As a result of being grafted in, we begin to read the Bible. We don't understand everything, but there are some things that start to penetrate and get ahold of us. Hebrews 4:12 says the Word is sharper than any two-edged sword. As we read the Word, it wounds, shapes, and molds us into the image of Christ.

The Word works within us until it becomes a natural part of our lives. I often used to think, *I can't do this. I can't do that.* And then I began to get hold of Romans 8:37, that says "I'm more than a conqueror." *I thought, well, you don't look like one. You don't act like one.* I would get up in the morning and look in the mirror. And I would say, "I don't look good at all, but thank you, Lord, I'm more than a conqueror." I kept saying it until I believed I was a conqueror, because that Word worked within my spirit and did not return void.

With the grafting comes the pruning. That same Word, that living and powerful and sharp sword, cuts and wounds you at times. To become who God designed you to be, He must cut and trim off those things that don't fit His image for you. Your new identity is forged as that sword of the Word cuts aside your fleshly thoughts and begins to implant spiritual thoughts. *"Every branch in Me that does not bear fruit He takes away; and every branch that bears fruit He prunes, that it may bear more fruit"* (John 15:2).

Let that Word come in and cut off the things of the world — whether it be smoking, drinking, sexual immorality, lying, cheating, gambling, whatever. Become the conqueror that the Word says you are. Let the Word come in and divide what your soul says and what the Spirit says. When you are more than a conqueror, you have dominion over these things. Put the devil under your feet, where he belongs! The way you undo the words the devil says about you is to follow Jesus's example: Say, "It is written." Don't give your opinion. Say what the Bible says about your situation — remember, your identity is what the Word says you are, not who or what the devil (or anybody else) says you are.

Chapter Two

The Gates of Authority in Your Identity — Part One

∴

In the book of Nehemiah, gates can represent places of authority in your identity. They are where you make decisions — which gates to open and which gates to close — whether you say "yes" or "no" to the enemy, and "yes" or "no" to God. Nehemiah tells of 12 gates, all but one of which are mentioned in the third chapter. The 12th gate is found in chapter eight, and it is a very unusual gate. Let's identify each of the gates to find out how they were built and when they should be open or shut.

The Sheep Gate

Then Eliashib the high priest rose up with his brethren the priests and built the Sheep Gate; they consecrated it and hung its doors. They built as far as the Tower of the Hundred, and consecrated it, then as far as the Tower of Hananel. (NEHEMIAH 3:1)

Why would the Sheep Gate be mentioned first? The Sheep Gate was where animals were brought into the city for sacrifice. In terms of our identities, this is where we first opened our hearts for Jesus to become our personal Savior. He is the Lamb of God who took our place and was sacrificed for our sins. Without the Sheep Gate, there could be no restoration of our identities.

Jesus is your personal Lamb and your personal Savior, but He is more than that. I traced the history of the sacrificed lamb to the Jews' departure from Egypt, when lambs were slaughtered on the doorsteps of all Jewish households. Afterwards, the blood of these lambs was put on the lintels and over the doorposts of their houses. When the angel of death passed over Egypt on the night of Passover,

The Gates of Authority in Your Identity — Part One

no death came to the households that were marked with the blood of lambs. Every family had a lamb. Jesus is the Lamb who was sacrificed for both you and your family! Jesus is also the Lamb for the nations. In Israel, the priests sacrificed a lamb every morning and every evening for the sins of their nation. There was a tremendous concern that Israel, as a nation, would only be able to serve the living God through daily atonement for any sin.

You keep your faith energized by acknowledging every good thing in you through Christ.

We say, "Is God just for the nation of Israel? Was He just for the Hebrew people?" No, God is for every nation. When John the Baptist saw Jesus in John 1:29, he said, "*Behold! The Lamb of God who takes away the sin of the world!*" Jesus is the Lamb for the salvation of the entire world. He is the one who makes it possible for believers of every nation to have identity restoration. He is the Lamb slain for you, your family, your nation, and the world.

Many different types of people were involved in building and repairing the Sheep Gate. Nehemiah chapter three says that both priests and laymen were involved. Eliashib, the high priest, helped hang this gate. His name means "God will restore." How true. God restores through Jesus, the Lamb. Note, though, that not just the leaders are responsible for hanging the Sheep Gate in the lives of unsaved people. You and I share that same responsibility of leading others to a relationship with the Lamb of God.

According to the Word, we have a responsibility to share our faith: *"That the sharing of your faith may become effective by the acknowledgment of every good thing which is in you in Christ Jesus"* (Philemon 1:6).

How do you make your faith effective? The word "effective" is from the Greek *energēs* which means "active, operative, effectual, and powerful." When God drops faith in your heart, your faith is energized. You keep your faith energized by acknowledging every good thing in you through Christ. What's in you? A new nature! What's in your new nature? The fruit of the Spirit are: *"Love, joy, peace, longsuffering, kindness, goodness, faithfulness, gentleness, self-control"* (Galatians 5:22–23). All of this came when you were grafted into Christ. When you demonstrate your new nature to those who knew you before you were saved, people will take notice because *"old things have passed away"* and *"all things have become new"* (2 Corinthians 5:17). Suddenly, you love everyone and you want everyone to experience the redemption of the Lamb.

The Fish Gate

Also the sons of Hassenaah built the Fish Gate; they laid its beams and hung its doors with its bolts and bars. (NEHEMIAH 3:3)

The second gate that is mentioned in the third chapter of Nehemiah is called the Fish Gate. The Hebrew word for "fish" means "squirming." That certainly describes a new Christian, doesn't it? A new believer squirms with excitement. They tend to say, "If I had been saved for as long as everyone else, I would have converted the whole world!" A new Christian wants to share the gospel with everyone because he is so full of new life.

Everyone is thrilled by each development of a newborn baby. With new Christians, it is no different.

Their enthusiasm is contagious. You see a new believer being baptized, and it is very precious; or you watch him witnessing to all of his friends and growing in the Lord every day. I love new Christians, for they bring to a congregation a special freshness that can be brought by no other person. As a new baby brings freshness to a home, so, too, does a new Christian to the body of Christ.

Never think of yourself as too noble to help newly converted believers.

Who built the Fish Gate? It is interesting that mostly "lay people" helped. Most of the workers were everyday people. But Nehemiah 3:5 says that the *"nobles did not put their shoulders to the work of their Lord."* In Nehemiah 3, the names of those who helped with the work were recorded in the Bible for all time. Those who did not, the nobles, were left out. You're never too "noble" to do the work that God has called you to do.

God wants the whole body of Christ to bless new Christians. We are all supposed to involve ourselves with the new ones. We are to love and encourage them and do as much as possible for them. Some people say, "That's a pastor's job." No, it is a job that was assigned by Jesus to everyone. Never think of yourself as too noble to help newly converted believers. Dedicate yourself to helping them grow in their walks with the Lord.

New Christians are weak and may not know all the benefits of kingdom living. It is up to all of us to encourage them in their struggles so that the devil can't sneak in and steal their new identity. They are God's "beloved," and like children, their loving Father isn't going to forsake them when they blow it or do wrong things. You and I must reassure them when the devil comes along and tries to tell them that God doesn't love them anymore, that God still loves them and wants to give them a victorious, abundant life. We must point them to Scripture and teach them how to fight their battles with the Word; we must help them grow in their faith so that they can, in turn, reach others.

The Old Gate

Moreover Jehoiada the son of Paseah and Meshullam the son of Besodeiah repaired the Old Gate; they laid its beams and hung its doors, with its bolts and bars. (NEHEMIAH 3:6)

Who wants an old gate? Most people want everything to be new! After all, aren't there enough burned materials in the walls without having an old gate, too? God has a special gate through which bad parts of your past, such as hurts and fears, must come out. He wants to remove those things, and He has a gate especially for that purpose.

There are some things in your past that God wants you to use to help other people. Sometimes you have received comfort, and God wants you to share that same comfort with another person. It is very important that we let God be in control of all the old things in our lives.

Who helped to hang the Old Gate and rebuild that section of the wall? Many, many people from all walks of life were involved. There were goldsmiths, merchants, rulers, and daughters. Women helped to

The Gates of Authority in Your Identity — Part One

hang the Old Gate, as did a group of people called the Gibeonites. I thought, "If anybody would know about rebuilding from a bad past, it would be a Gibeonite!" Perhaps you are not familiar with the Gibeonites, but they turned out to be some of my favorite people in the Bible. Initially, they are found in the book of Joshua, where they lived up to their reputations from Joshua's time. They were originally deceivers.

The problem was that the Gibeonites had not really traveled from a far country; in fact, they lived right there in Canaan!

In Joshua chapter nine, you find a group of Gibeonites telling Joshua and his princes, "We have traveled a great distance to this land." These people had long beards, old, ragged clothes, moldy wineskins, and a very dirty appearance. They told Joshua, "We have heard about your mighty God. We heard that He killed your enemies Sihon and Og and parted the Red Sea. We have traveled a great distance so that we can make a covenant with you."

God had warned Joshua, "Don't make a covenant with any of the Canaanites." Since Joshua thought the Gibeonites were not from Canaan, Joshua agreed that a covenant could be established.

The problem was that the Gibeonites had not really traveled from a far country; in fact, they lived right there in Canaan! But they had heard the report that Joshua would conquer all the land of Canaan, feared it, and believed it. They even went to great lengths of deception to be a part of it!

Joshua and his princes never prayed about the situation. They simply entered into a covenant with the Gibeonites: "We won't hurt each other. We will stand up for each other and even fight for each other." Everything was all set and ready to go because of the Gibeonites' deception of the Israelites.

If only Joshua had known the Gibeonites' history! Originally, the Gibeonites were called Hivites, and Hivite means "snake." The book of Genesis tells us that Jacob had a daughter, Dinah, who was raped by a Hivite man named Shechem. Afterward, he went home and told his father, "I want to marry Dinah."

Shechem's father told Jacob the whole story and then asked, "What must I do for my son to marry

The Gates of Authority in Your Identity — Part One

your daughter?" Jacob's sons said, "All of the Hivite males must become as we are. Your men must all be circumcised."

The Hivites were willing, so all of the men were circumcised. But while they were still recovering, two sons of Jacob, Simeon and Levi, Dinah's brothers, raced in and killed all of the men in revenge. Jacob was so upset and ashamed of his sons' behavior that he and his family had to leave the country. Simeon and Levi had deceived the Hivites, but bread cast on the water always returns. In the book of Joshua, the sons of the Hivites now deceived the sons of Jacob!

Three days after the Israelites had made a covenant with the Gibeonites, Joshua discovered their deception. Three days is always the number of resurrection — Joshua and his men were resurrected all right; they had their eyes opened! The Israelites marched into Gibeon and said, "You lied to us!"

The Gibeonites admitted, "It's true, but we were afraid." Joshua was very disturbed. He consulted the rulers, who said, "We cannot break a covenant. But we can punish the Gibeonites by making them serve by carrying water and cutting wood for the congregation and the altar of the Lord."

The Gibeonites became servants to the Israelites, and shortly afterward, their covenant was put to a test. All of Canaan heard about the covenant between Gibeon and Israel. They said, "We are going to go down and fight against Gibeon." So, the Gibeonites sent word to Joshua and asked for help.

Joshua prayed, "God, what should I do?" I'm glad that he prayed this time. He should have prayed the first time, and he wouldn't have been in this mess! God told Joshua, "Go out because you will win the battle."

As the Canaanites battled against Israel and Gibeon, the night began to fall. Joshua knew that if darkness came too soon, Israel would lose the battle. He was such a man of faith that he said, *"Sun, stand still over Gibeon; and Moon, in the valley of Aijalon"* (Joshua 10:12). God honored Joshua's words; the sky remained light, and Israel won the battle for the Gibeonites.

We say, "God, why did you win a battle for the people of Gibeon? They were liars and deceivers!"

But God says, "They were new converts. I always have special miracles for new converts."

The Gates of Authority in Your Identity — Part One

I would venture to say that the chapter about this battle is the greatest miracle chapter in the Old Testament, and it displays God's love for new converts to the faith. But this story has an even happier ending. The Gibeonites show up later in the book of Ezra as one of the first groups returning to build the temple in Jerusalem. But they are no longer called Gibeonites; they are called Nethinim, which means "given ones." They were given to duty. They became the temple assistants in ancient Jerusalem.

When we are weak, He is strong! He designed us to reign in our weaknesses.

No matter how bad the Gibeonites' past may have looked, God forgave them and brought them into victory. They knew that God forgave bad pasts. God also wants to take your past and make it a blessing because you are His beloved child. He knows that the devil will come along to try to deceive you and lie to you. He also knows you are weak. When you begin to believe the devil's lies and think you aren't strong enough to do something, or when you feel you aren't smart enough, or even ask, "Why am I here?", that's when God comes to the rescue because you have a covenant with Him. God says He gives strength to the weak, as Paul can attest to: [God said] " *'My grace is sufficient for you, for My strength is made perfect in weakness.' Therefore most gladly I will rather boast in my infirmities, that the power of Christ may rest upon me"* (2 Corinthians 12:9). When we are weak, He is strong! He designed us to reign in our weaknesses.

The Valley Gate

Hanun and the inhabitants of Zanoah repaired the Valley Gate. They built it, hung its doors with its bolts and bars, and repaired a thousand cubits of the wall as far as the Refuse Gate. (NEHEMIAH 3:13)

While on his inspection tour of the wall, Nehemiah stopped at the Valley Gate on his third night in Jerusalem. This gate represents God's first miracle in your life — rescuing you from hell. He has rescued your identity, your body, and your spirit from hell by building the Valley Gate in your life.

The Gates of Authority in Your Identity — Part One

I looked to see who built the Valley Gate and discovered that the people of the whole town of Zanoah were involved. Everyone is involved in taking people out of hell. Everybody! The whole body of Christ should be praying, seeking God, and asking Him to pour out His Spirit so that we can rescue others from the torment of hell.

John the Baptist was totally committed to rescuing people. He preached a baptism of repentance for the remission of sins. In doing so, he was fulfilling the words of Isaiah:

> *"The voice of one crying in the wilderness:*
> *'Prepare the way of the LORD;*
> *Make His paths straight.*
> ***Every valley shall be filled***
> *And every mountain and hill brought low;*
> *The crooked places shall be made straight*
> *And the rough ways smooth;*
> *And all flesh shall see the salvation of God.'"*
> **(LUKE 3:4-6, EMPHASIS ADDED)**

Valleys are sometimes used figuratively to denote a condition of loneliness and danger. What could be more lonely or dangerous than hell? It is so disturbing to think of all the lost souls in the world. Yet God, working through the body of Christ, can indeed fill every valley, bring down mountains and hills, straighten crooked places, and smooth out rough ways in order to bring salvation to all flesh! In our own strength, it won't happen, but because He reigns in our weakness, nothing is impossible.

The whole body of Christ is involved in rescuing people from hell.

I love to witness on airplanes and have always enjoyed personal soul winning. I remember one time my daughter and I prayed about a certain flight; we agreed that I would be able to witness to someone. I boarded my plane in a state of exhaustion and said, "Lord, you have to open this door. I'm surely not going to knock it down." Isn't that silly? After all, God always has to open the doors for us. We never knock doors down!

I exchanged a few casual words with the man sitting next to me, and then, out of the clear blue sky, he said, "I just love to talk about religion." He really had

The Gates of Authority in Your Identity — Part One

my attention! I said, "I do, too." And before that man reached his destination, he had prayed and invited Jesus Christ into his heart. The whole body of Christ is involved in rescuing people from hell. Watch and pray for opportunities. Who knows, maybe today God will use you to help hang the Valley Gate in someone's life.

The Dung Gate

> *Malchijah the son of Rechab, leader of the district of Beth Haccerem, repaired the Refuse Gate; he built it and hung its doors with its bolts and bars.* (NEHEMIAH 3:14)

Everyone knows that refuse is garbage, but why would God have anything to do with it? God has a refuse gate through which he removes the junk from your life. We must be sure to keep this gate open when God wants to remove something.

I looked to see who was involved in hanging the Refuse Gate and found that a ruler hung the gate. Why would a man of authority fulfill this task? It is because God doesn't want us all dragging up garbage from other people's lives. When someone has fallen away from the truth, the Bible says that those *"who are spiritual restore such a one . . ."* (Galatians 6:1).

That's what happened after David committed adultery with Bathsheba. This sin gave *"great occasion to the enemies of the Lord to blaspheme"* (2 Samuel 12:14), so it was imperative to rectify it. Though David tried to cover up his sin, God revealed it to Nathan, who confronted David. God didn't want to annihilate David; He wanted to restore David. When David realized this, he repented wholeheartedly. In fact, he even wrote Psalm 51, describing the mercy and love of God that opened the Refuse Gate in his life and brought about his total restoration.

I appreciate the people in our church who stay away from the trash in other people's lives. Instead, they go to a pastor and make him aware of any negative situations. They respect that correction should come from one who is in spiritual authority. When God wants to take garbage out of your life, open the gate of your heart. However, when others want to bring garbage into your life, keep the gate closed.

The Gates of Authority in Your Identity — Part One

The Fountain Gate

Shallun the son of Col-Hozeh, leader of the district of Mizpah, repaired the Fountain Gate; he built it, covered it, hung its doors with its bolts and bars, and repaired the wall of the Pool of Shelah by the King's Garden, as far as the stairs that go down from the City of David. (NEHEMIAH 3:15)

The Fountain Gate has a long, detailed description; I personally believe that this gate represents the baptism in the Holy Spirit. It delights me to think that God has a Fountain Gate to refresh the life of every believer.

Some people say, "We have the Holy Spirit at the new birth." But God doesn't want us just *having* the Holy Spirit; He wants us *overflowing* with the Holy Spirit! The Holy Spirit wants to be a refreshing fountain in our lives that just keeps giving and giving of His blessings.

Some believers close the Fountain Gate. They say, "I don't want to be baptized with the Holy Spirit."

But every Christian needs to keep this gate open to God. After all, He put this gate in our identities.

I looked at the description of the Fountain Gate and saw that a ruler's son built it and set up the doors, locks, and bars. But after this, many different people were involved in repairing and rebuilding the wall. In the same way, God pours out the Holy Spirit onto many different kinds of people — no matter their denomination or tradition.

The baptism in the Holy Spirit is what opened and transformed my identity.

In Joel 2:28, God said, *"It shall come to pass afterward that I will pour out My Spirit on all flesh . . ."* That includes you. Don't close off your identity to the Fountain Gate. It is one of the greatest helps that God has provided for your life.

A good friend of mine has always had a warm, wonderful, and gracious personality; but before being baptized in the Holy Spirit, she had a hard time saying, "I'm sorry." But after she received the baptism in the Holy Spirit, her new, improved, Spirit-filled identity became radiant!

The Gates of Authority in Your Identity — Part One

Before I was baptized in the Holy Spirit, I could never testify for the Lord. Once at a church service, I was asked to share a testimony. The only thing I could say was, "I'm glad I'm here." When I sat down, my husband-to-be nudged me and whispered, "You're a liar." It was true! I was not glad to be there because I did not enjoy fellowship with other Christians. The baptism in the Holy Spirit is what opened and transformed my identity.

Another thing to note is that when you follow people in the Bible, the Holy Spirit played a huge role in the formation of their identities and in the fulfillment of their destinies. In John the Baptist's case, the Spirit spoke to his father and told him that he would have a son and *"He will also be filled with the Holy Spirit, even from his mother's womb"* (Luke 1:15). His identity was formed by the Holy Spirit while he was still in the womb (see also Luke 1:41, 44).

In other instances, the Spirit came upon others to empower them to do specific things. Though Samson wasn't filled with the Spirit in the womb, the Spirit did come upon him later in life: *"And the Spirit of the LORD began to move upon him at Mahaneh Dan between Zorah and Eshtaol"* (Judges 13:25). Samson's identity was to subdue the Philistines who were oppressing Israel at the time.

Another man was named Bezalel. God told Moses that he had filled Bezalel specifically to create the various items needed for the tabernacle:

> Then the LORD spoke to Moses, saying: "See, I have called by name Bezalel the son of Uri, the son of Hur, of the tribe of Judah. And I have filled him with the Spirit of God, in wisdom, in understanding, in knowledge, and in all manner of workmanship, to design artistic works, to work in gold, in silver, in bronze, in cutting jewels for setting, in carving wood, and to work in all manner of workmanship." (EXODUS 31:1-5)

The Spirit gave him the skills and abilities to become the master craftsman that he was, which enabled him to craft all the various "masterpieces" required in serving the Lord in the tabernacle. Yes, God provided him with other helpers, "gifted artisans," to make all that the Lord commanded Moses, everything from the tabernacle itself to the mercy seat, the utensils, lampstands, priestly garments and more! As their leader, Bezalel was filled with the Spirit to accomplish the tasks.

When you feel attacked by identity problems, pray in the Spirit.

Likewise, your identity is maximized when you are filled with the Spirit. Your identity goes along with your destiny. God has a plan for your life. He has given you gifts and talents, but when you get filled with the Holy Spirit, it does something special to what He has already put in you. It makes what He's already put in you supernatural. I believe that's why I'm so strong — not just some weak, old lady! I'm being filled with the Spirit and praying in the Spirit every day. Why? Because it makes you supernatural. The anointing of the Spirit takes what's inside and makes you supernatural!

When you feel attacked by identity problems, pray in the Spirit. You will find that your identity will then receive brand new strength as the power of the Holy Spirit flows through you.

The Prison Gate

> *Palal the son of Uzai made repairs opposite the buttress, and on the tower which projects from the king's upper house that was by the court of the prison. After him Pedaiah the son of Parosh made repairs.* (NEHEMIAH 3:25)

Gate number six is called the Prison Gate, and it symbolizes all the areas where we have been in bondage. Some of us have been imprisoned by habits, and others have been held captive by worry. But whatever the prisons are, God wants to free us from them.

We open the Prison Gate to remove wrong bondages, but then we must close it and imprison ourselves to God's will. God wants our wills bound to Him in faithfulness. He also wants us bound in faithfulness to the body of Christ. It is in taking the identity of a bondservant that you will find your greatest freedom in Christ.

God does not want us running around telling everyone else how to be free. He wants to free us Himself. He is to be the ruler of our lives.

Chapter Three

The Gates of Authority in Your Identity — Part Two

:::

It's exciting that God has placed gates in our identities to indicate places of authority. These gates are where we make decisions — for God or for the enemy.

We have learned that there are fountains of water near the gates, so we can put out fiery darts with God's Word. Towers near all the gates symbolize where the Holy Spirit watches to help guide and direct your decisions of when to keep the gates of your identity open or closed.

So far we have discussed the Sheep Gate, the Fish Gate, the Old Gate, the Valley Gate, the Dung Gate, the Fountain Gate, and the Prison Gate. The next gate is a very special one through which God brings His Word into our lives.

The Water Gate

Moreover the Nethinim who dwelt in Ophel made repairs as far as the place in front of the Water Gate toward the east, and on the projecting tower. (NEHEMIAH 3:26)

The Water Gate was essential to the Israelites, for through this gate came the city's water supply. The people couldn't just turn on a tap and have handy all the water they needed!

The builders of the wall up to the Water Gate were Nethinim — you know who they were! They were the ancient Gibeonites, or Hivites, whose new name meant "those set apart" or "the given ones." God brings special people into your life to carry His Word into your heart, doesn't He?

When God brings people to carry His Word into your heart, don't close the gate, or you will shut out refreshment. Water refreshes you, and it also cleanses you. You can look into water and see the

The Gates of Authority in Your Identity — Part Two

image of your face because water is like a mirror, producing a picture of what you look like. In that way, God's Word shows you exactly where you stand with God and others.

The Water Gate must be open to God's Word and not to false doctrine. Many times, young Christians become concerned about whether they are receiving the right feeding. True, some are led into false doctrine, but I have noticed that the Holy Spirit is very protective of baby Christians to see that they receive the living Word.

Years ago, when we were holding church meetings in a store building, my husband and I were involved in an Oral Roberts city-wide campaign for Christ. As personal workers in the campaign, we received a list of new converts who were living in our area.

My husband personally called on those people and invited them to our church. We had just started a revival meeting, and four of the families that we invited came to that meeting. Remember, they were all brand-new Christians who were probably only a week old in the Lord.

I was, of course, eager for the service to be just right for our visitors. Everything went well until the evangelist stood up to minister, and five men walked into the church and slammed the door behind them. They had everyone's attention — how could you help but notice them?

When the evangelist began to speak, the men were up-and-down, one after another, to go to the men's room. I thought, "Do they have kidney trouble, or what?" Then one man stood up in the middle of the teaching and began to prophesy. "In the name of Jeremiah!" He started running down an aisle, but the evangelist stopped him and said sharply, "We don't care to hear anything in the name of Jeremiah. We are here in the name of Jesus. Sit down! You are out of order."

We really had some spooks at that service! That night, I was very upset about the situation. I told my husband, "Here were four families of brand-new Christians who will probably never come back. They probably think we are a church of nuts, and I wouldn't blame them at all."

We prayed, and then we visited the families. As we drove to see them, the Lord sweetly assured me that He was working in all of these people's lives.

He would protect them from being offended by the previous night's incident.

At the first family's home, they were very excited about the Lord. The father said, "We really enjoyed the service last night, but then when the men stood up, we had the strangest feeling that something was wrong."

I thought, *These are the Lord's little babies. He is protecting them and causing them to discern the truth with the guard tower of His Holy Spirit.* God is watching to see that baby Christians get the true Word! And the best part of the story is that we did not lose one family. God's Word can also be a discerner of truth in your life.

The Horse Gate

> *Beyond the Horse Gate the priests made repairs, each in front of his own house.*
> **(NEHEMIAH 3:28)**

Why would you need a horse gate? In Jerusalem, it was for carrying burdens in and out of the city. You know, God wants any wrong burdens out of your life.

Cares are wrong burdens that He wants you to cast on Him, *"casting all your care upon Him, for He cares for you"* (1 Peter 5:7). But at the same time, we are to help bear one another's burdens by praying for each other.

Sometimes we carry people's cares on ourselves without taking them to the Lord, and that isn't right. The role of the intercessor is key in the kingdom of God, but we must remember that *"It is Christ who died, and furthermore is also risen, who is even at the right hand of God, who also makes intercession for us"* (Romans 8:34).

When you bring prayers and present them to God, you do so through the sacrificial blood of Jesus Christ.

When Paul was encouraging Timothy to fight the good fight, he exhorted him: *"first of all that supplications, prayers, intercessions, and giving of thanks be made for all men . . . for this is good and acceptable in the sight of God our Savior"* (1 Timothy 2:1, 3). All men? Really? That could become a real burden! So, the Horse Gate symbolizes that you should not become overburdened by either your own cares or the cares of others. You can minister actively to the body of Christ by bearing their burdens in prayer and by being a vessel through which the Holy Spirit flows, but you don't have to take everyone's cares upon yourself.

Sometimes people in the ministry feel overburdened because they hear problems, problems, problems all day. Unless they remember to take those burdens to the Lord, the load can become too heavy and cause the ministers to break.

Who was involved in building the wall beyond the Horse Gate? The priests were involved. Does that mean the laity doesn't have to bear any burdens? No, it doesn't, because the New Testament calls you chosen, holy, and a priest of the Lord (see 1 Peter 2:9). You are called to minister as a priest before Him by praying for others. A priest is one who intercedes for the people and makes sacrifices. When you bring prayers and present them to God, you do so through the sacrificial blood of Jesus Christ.

The Lord saw that it was important for you to have a horse gate in your life. It is important that you use it to help bear people's burdens through the priesthood of prayer. This is essential to the completion of your identity. People who don't care about anyone getting saved, except their own families, are off the mark. God gave you this part of your identity to help you carry burdens from other people's lives, as well as carry them from your own, to the Lord.

The East Gate

. . . After him Shemaiah the son of Shechaniah, the keeper of the East Gate, made repairs. (NEHEMIAH 3:29)

Only one man, Shemaiah, built the East Gate, and he was the gate's keeper. The East Gate, now known as the Golden Gate, which is directly across from the Mount of Olives, is the gate through which our Lord Jesus Christ will return to Jerusalem in His second coming. It is believed that He passed through this gate on His way to Calvary. This gate in your heart is to create expectancy and hope as you look for the return of Jesus. When you lose contact with Jesus's promise to return, you lose comfort and strength. The Bible says that we find comfort knowing that Jesus is coming again for us (1 Thessalonians 4:15–18).

The Gates of Authority in Your Identity — Part Two

The East Gate is closely guarded by the Holy Spirit so that only the living Christ can enter it. No wonder Jesus warned, *"Many will come in My name, saying, 'I am the Christ,' and will deceive many"* (Matthew 24:5). He wants the gate closed to anyone but Him. Jesus said, *"But of that day and hour no one knows, not even the angels of heaven, but My Father only"* (Matthew 24:36). Only the Father in Heaven, the keeper of the East Gate, knows when the Messiah will come back. But we have been told to live each day as though it were the day of Christ's blessed return.

The Miphkad Gate

After him Malchijah, one of the goldsmiths, made repairs as far as the house of the Nethinim and of the merchants, in front of the Miphkad Gate, and as far as the upper room at the corner. And between the upper room at the corner, as far as the Sheep Gate, the goldsmiths and the merchants made repairs. (NEHEMIAH 3:31-32)

The eleventh gate found in Nehemiah chapter three is the *Miphkad* gate. *Miphkad* means "assignment." God has a special assigned place for each of His people. He didn't say, "You're saved, so now just hang loose." He said, "I have designed a plan for your life."

God's plan for you was meant to make you productive and a blessing to those whose lives cross yours.

Many people think this is predestination, but predestination means something different. Romans 8:29 says, *"Whom He foreknew, He also predestined to be conformed to the image of His Son, that He might be the firstborn among many brethren."*

You were not predestined to be saved or lost. That is not predestination because 2 Peter 3:9 says that it isn't God's will that any person should perish. God, being omniscient, knows every person's decision, but He does not predestine your salvation or lack of salvation. Becoming a Christian is an individual decision. But God says, "My predestination for Christians is that they be conformed to the image of my Son." This is God's desire and plan for all believers.

The Gates of Authority in Your Identity — Part Two

God's assignment, or *Miphkad,* concerns your individual life. Don't think you're just an accident. God drew out a plan for your life in particular. What if you don't flow in that plan? Then you miss it, but you don't lose your salvation. Many Christians miss God's plan for their lives, but God still has that plan for them. We must be obedient to seek God's will so that we can flow in our assignments. God's plan for you was meant to make you productive and a blessing to those whose lives cross yours.

You have to be sensitive and open toward God for His plan, because sometimes He calls you to do something that may seem uncomfortable. He may lead you into something where you tell Him, "This isn't my thing at all!"

Once when my husband and I were new in the ministry, we were invited to be assistant pastors in a large Pentecostal church in Amarillo, Texas. I had heard that the church had a beautiful parsonage for the assistant pastors, and I thought, *Wouldn't that be great?* Wasn't that a high spiritual motivation?

After we arrived to live in Amarillo, my husband and I were informed, "In all our church history, we have never done this, but we have hired two full-time assistant pastors. The other young couple is expecting a baby, and you don't have any children, so we are putting them in the parsonage."

The greatest blow to my life as a young wife had been when my doctors said, "You cannot have a baby," so the statement about our childless state stung deeply. Then I found that our new home was to be a tiny apartment that was also being called "home" by mice and cockroaches. It was grubby and dirty, so the pastor said, "I'll give you some paint."

Immediately, I had no leading for us to stay in Amarillo as assistant pastors. I had no leading at all! This could not be God's *Miphkad* Gate for me, so I slammed it shut as hard as I could slam it. But my husband would not do the same. He said, "Marilyn, I told the Lord that I would go through any door He opened. I believe that He has opened this door, and I am going to go through it."

"And live here?"

"Yes."

"With the salary so low?"

"With the salary so low. This is God's place for us."

My husband helped me chase out mice and cockroaches, and we painted and cleaned the apartment.

The Gates of Authority in Your Identity — Part Two

Amarillo was miserably hot, and the apartment was miserably small, so after a few weeks, I told my husband, "I think you should resign."

He said, "No, the Lord has led us here."

I warned, "If you don't resign, I will leave." So, I left Wally and went home to my mother. I told her, "It's too awful in Amarillo. I can't stay there." She was so sweet. She said nothing condemning, but I know that she prayed.

The Holy Spirit knows how to lead you in and how to lead you out. Look to Him and trust Him, and then you can receive the best results in your life.

Then one day, I opened my Bible to the book of Revelation, and a Scripture practically jumped off the page: *"I have set before you an open door, and no one can shut it"* (Revelation 3:8).

I quickly closed my Bible but was nagged by the thought, *Have I closed the gate to God?* Yet God seemed to be saying, "I am holding it open, and you *will* walk through it."

I thought, *So I opened my Bible to a Scripture. No big deal, it doesn't mean anything.*

The next day, an acquaintance of my mother's called and said, "The Lord has strongly impressed a Scripture on my heart for Marilyn."

My mother told the woman, "You talk with her," and she handed me the telephone. The woman told me that she had a Scripture for me, and I asked, "What is it?" dreading that it might be the same Scripture in Revelation. And it was.

> . . . God is using all kinds of identities to cause you to flow with His will. It is His will that you flow in a particular assignment that He designed.

I said, "Lord, I give up," packed my bags, and went home to my husband and the church in Amarillo. You probably wonder how it all turned out. It was one of the most delightful times of my life.

My husband and I worked hard, and we saw God move mightily in our lives. We held early morning prayer meetings and set up a visitation program. God opened a door for me to teach a class of young

The Gates of Authority in Your Identity — Part Two

married people, and the class doubled, tripled, and quadrupled. Marriages that had been broken up were wonderfully reconciled. I became very excited about the Bible because so much study was required in order to teach an adult class. Through that study, I gained my first great desire to teach God's Word.

I had experienced difficulty accepting the *Miphkad* Gate that God opened for us in Amarillo, but when God opened the gate once again for us to leave, it was even more difficult. We had fallen in love with the assignment God had given us.

The Holy Spirit knows how to lead you in and how to lead you out. Look to Him and trust Him, and then you can receive the best results in your life.

Malchijah, a goldsmith, made repairs as far as the house of the Nethinim and of the merchants, in front of the *Miphkad* Gate. Isn't that interesting? All kinds of people are used by God in causing you to flow in His divine plan. Have strangers ever been used by God to get you into God's plan? They have in my life.

Once, I was flying to Buffalo, New York, and the plane I traveled on was prevented from landing in Buffalo due to a ground storm. I thought, *Oh no, I am going to be late to speak at the luncheon.*

We had to land in Rochester, and I boarded the slowest bus that I have ever ridden. Midway to Buffalo, the bus driver stopped to change for another driver. I was really beginning to feel panicky when the man seated across from me looked over and said, "Looks like you're going to miss your lunch today, doesn't it?"

I said, "It really does."

Then he said, "Well, they will be waiting when you get there." When the man spoke those words, the Holy Spirit confirmed them, "That's right. They will be waiting." I arrived two hours late, and when I walked in where the luncheon would be held, the hostess came rushing over to me. She said, "You are just in time. The hotel mixed up our luncheon times! We were supposed to eat at 12:30, but they scheduled us for 1:30. We have just finished the last course."

I want to assure you that today, God is using all kinds of identities to cause you to flow with His will. It is His will that you flow in a particular assignment that He designed. In doing so, you will find yourself being the most effective, fulfilled Christian you can be.

The Gates of Authority in Your Identity — Part Two

The Ephraim Gate

The last gate is the Ephraim Gate, which is found in Nehemiah 8:16:

> *Then the people went out and brought them [branches] and made themselves booths, each one on the roof of his house, or in their courtyards or the courts of the house of God, and in the open square of the Water Gate and in the open square of the Gate of Ephraim.*

The Ephraim Gate is the "double fruit" gate. The Bible does not tell you who hangs this gate, but I think that the person responsible for hanging it is you. We may wonder, *Does God want me to be doubly fruitful?* Oh, yes, He wants you to have a double portion and be doubly blessed. In the book of Deuteronomy, you find that a double portion of inheritance was always given to the firstborn. Jesus is God's firstborn, and we are His body, so God has a double portion of inheritance for us.

You ask, "Why don't I have it?" James 4:2 says, *"You do not have because you do not ask."* In Matthew chapter eight, a centurion sought Jesus to heal his sick servant and said, *"Lord, I am not worthy that You should come under my roof. But only speak a word, and my servant will be healed"* (v. 8).

Jesus then marveled and said, "I have not seen faith this great in all Israel." Then He told the man, *"As you have believed, so let it be done for you"* (v. 13). You get that for which you believe! And the centurion's servant was healed at that very hour.

Double fruit? God says, "You'll get it, if you believe me for it." But nobody can hang your Ephraim Gate for you. You have to hang it yourself by faith.

If you want big things, you start with little things. Believe for each step in the process. God will verify in your heart what He wants you to do . . .

Faith is a process. Many times, people think they can just jump right into something big when they do not have the experience, skills, or talents. They may not even have God's leading to do it in the first place. I didn't get to the point where I could have a healing meeting attended by over 1 million people in

The Gates of Authority in Your Identity — Part Two

Pakistan without 40 years of God's leading, guiding, and directing me step-by-step. If you want big things, you start with little things. Believe for each step in the process. God will verify in your heart what He wants you to do, then you begin to speak it — speak the promises in God's Word — and believe them. Start seeing it come to pass through faith.

It will be exciting to see what God does in the years to come for this amazing nation and the people there.

My faith was recently rewarded. I had believed for decades that I would be able to go to Saudi Arabia and have a healing meeting there. When things began to look promising, COVID-19 hit. But I didn't give up. I kept believing for "double fruit" — first, getting into Saudi Arabia, then beginning the process of holding a healing meeting for the precious people in Saudi Arabia. God answered those years of prayers, and I was finally able to get into Saudi Arabia in October of 2021. In the process of getting into the country and while I was there, I saw God work one miracle after another. He even set in motion the wheels for future healing ministry into Saudi Arabia. I do not know exactly what this will look like or when it will take place, but God has connected me with people inside Saudi Arabia who are hungry for God and desperate to receive God's healing touch. It will be exciting to see what God does in the years to come for this amazing nation and the people there.

Now, is this process over? No! But once I got through the Ephraim Gate, the process could move forward, step-by-step, according to God's plans. I can't wait to see what He has in store!

Chapter Four

Overcoming the Enemy of Your Identity

:::

The snake that appeared in the garden of Eden hasn't changed. He is a liar. First of all, he lies about who God says you are. He will tell you that God doesn't love you, that He's unhappy with you, that you don't do things the right way, you are a failure, and on and on he goes with his lies. He doesn't tell you that God is a loving Father. He doesn't point out that God so loved the world that He gave His most precious possession, His Son, to die for you. He lies about who you are. He messes with your identity and wants you to believe his lies so that you won't be able to fulfill God's call on your life.

Furthermore, the devil is a deceiver, and he is out to deceive you and me. The Bible tells us that his first attack was against a family. He deceived Adam and Eve into eating the forbidden fruit. Then he went after their sons, Cain and Abel. Both sons had heard of the blood sacrifice which Abel brought. But Cain didn't receive it and brought the food he had raised. The devil had deceived him into bringing what he thought was best. But it wasn't. Cain brought the work of his own hands, and that is never enough; you can never do enough to reach God in your own efforts. That's the devil's deception, his big lie. It's the blood that made Abel's sacrifice better. We are complete in Christ because of His shed blood on the cross. In jealousy and anger, Cain rose up and killed his brother. But God didn't close the book on humanity. Another son was born to Adam and Eve; Seth was the son of promise, from whose line the Messiah would come.

Revealing Satan's Strategies

Reading through the Bible reveals just how much Satan hates mankind. After instigating the fall of mankind, look at what he did to innocent Job. Job remained faithful to God, and God restored and even doubled all that he had lost. Satan even tried to corrupt the seed of mankind through whom the Messiah would come. Satan didn't want us to be redeemed. That's how much he hated us. That's when the fallen angels started cohabiting with women and corrupting humanity's seed with angelic seed. Humanity's seed had become so tainted that by the time God decided to send the flood, only Noah's family seed was found to be uncorrupted. God was determined to have a Savior and preserved a pure line from which Jesus would come.

But Satan was mad he hadn't won. Following the flood, Satan made his move to corrupt the whole of society. The Tower of Babel, located in what would become Babylon, became the origin of the occult. It started with men all speaking the same language, saying, "Let us build a tower to reach into heaven and make a name for ourselves" (see Genesis 11:4).

God decided to end that project by confusing their language and scattered the people over the face of the earth.

Guess who lived in that area. Abraham! Abraham was from Ur of the Chaldeans, in other words, Babylon; he was also an idolator. And again, God showed up. He took Abraham out of Babylon, and later promised that all of mankind would be blessed through Abraham's seed — the Jews, God's chosen people. They have been the focus of Satan's strategy ever since. Down through the ages, the Jews have been subjected to severe persecution because the devil was determined to destroy THE Seed that would destroy him.

Fast forward to Jesus. Satan's strategy was to kill Jesus. Yet God's overwhelming love for humanity brought his plans to naught. In fact, it was his biggest mistake because Jesus didn't stay dead! He rose from the dead! Hallelujah! Therein lies your victory over the enemy as well! Jesus has made you victorious!

Overcoming the Enemy of Your Identity

Exposing Satan's Tricks

That is good news since anyone who follows Jesus is now Satan's enemy. Never forget that in Jesus, you are victorious! You will find that you enter a war zone when God starts building the gates and walls of your identity, and some of the battles seem impossible to win. You think, *I can't hang in there any longer! It's just getting worse all the time.*

Never forget — you are on "team Jesus" and have already won!

In the day in which we live, it's obvious the devil is working overtime to get people to think less of themselves than what God thinks of them. The occult is running rampant. Addictions are at an all-time high. When you turn on the TV or watch a movie, you see demonic forces at work. The occult (witchcraft, astrology, new age, etc.) leads to death because anything instigated by Satan brings death. Nothing's changed. He's still the snake in the garden.

I don't want you to fall into any of his traps. That's why I want to help you see some of the things the enemy is trying to do. The devil needs to be exposed for who he is. Furthermore, you need to truly believe and understand the power that you have in the name of Jesus to overcome him. Never forget — you are on "team Jesus" and have already won!

Ridicule

You need to be super aware of the forces around you. I want to show you some of the enemy's tricks, but even better — I want to look at how you can overcome them. You know, the devil hasn't changed; he isn't very original. You can see the same attacks on Nehemiah's building of the wall as you will see in the building of your identity. In Nehemiah chapter four, the battle begins:

> *But it so happened, when Sanballat heard that we were rebuilding the wall, that he was furious and very indignant, and mocked the Jews. And he spoke before his brethren and the army of Samaria, and said, "What are these feeble Jews doing? Will they fortify themselves? Will they offer sacrifices? Will*

Overcoming the Enemy of Your Identity

they complete it in a day? Will they revive the stones from the heaps of rubbish — stones that are burned?" Now Tobiah the Ammonite was beside him, and he said, "Whatever they build, if even a fox goes up on it, he will break down their stone wall." (NEHEMIAH 4:1-3)

If you recall, Nehemiah's arrival in Jerusalem upset Sanballat terribly. Sanballat said, "Here is someone who cares about the welfare of the Israelites." The devil hates anyone who cares about God's people. He doesn't want you to live abundantly, and he certainly does not want your identity to be complete. The enemy hates and fears the work of the Holy Spirit in your life.

Sometimes ridicule is harder to take than outright verbal abuse!

Sanballat began to mock Nehemiah. He said, "Ha-ha. You think you're going to do something here? Forget it!" Then Sanballat's friend said, "There's nothing to that wall; a fox could knock it over." The enemy will tell you, "You can't change. Are you crazy? You've always been a failure." I think that one of the most difficult persecutions is laughter. Sometimes ridicule is harder to take than outright verbal abuse! When someone scorns the Lord's work in your life, just remember that the devil isn't trying any new tricks. He wants to reverse the upward swing in your identity. Don't take it! Just say, "Satan, I am not ignorant of your devices, and I will not allow them to continue." The Bible tells you exactly how Nehemiah handled every enemy attack. Nehemiah prayed:

> *Hear, O our God, for we are despised; turn their reproach on their own heads, and give them as plunder to a land of captivity! Do not cover their iniquity, and do not let their sin be blotted out from before You; for they have provoked You to anger before the builders. So we built the wall, and the entire wall was joined together up to half its height, for the people had a mind to work.* (NEHEMIAH 4:4-6)

Overcoming the Enemy of Your Identity

Scorn and mockery from the enemy were overcome by prayer and people who had "a mind to work." They were all in agreement: "Let's get the job done." Sometimes we work hard but we don't pray. Other times we pray a lot but don't work. We have to overcome the enemy with both of these. When Satan comes with mocking words, just pray and keep on working.

Conspiracy

The enemy's next evil device to sideline Nehemiah was conspiracy:

> *Now it happened, when Sanballat, Tobiah, the Arabs, the Ammonites, and the Ashdodites heard that the walls of Jerusalem were being restored and the gaps were beginning to be closed, that they became very angry, and all of them conspired together to come and attack Jerusalem and create confusion.*
> (NEHEMIAH 4:7-8)

When "Plan A" failed, all the enemies gathered and put their heads together. They said, "We're mad! We're going to devise a secret plan to get those Israelites and stop them from working." The devil has a plan to undo the work of God in your life. But you can overcome the conspiracies of the enemy through prayer: *"Nevertheless we made our prayer to our God, and because of them we set a watch against them day and night"* (Nehemiah 4:9).

> When enemies are conspiring against your plan, the first thing you should do is fall on your knees and pray.

It is interesting to note how many times you find prayer in the book of Nehemiah. Prayer is a key weapon against the enemy's tactics because it gets your eyes off the problem and puts them on God. In Nehemiah 4:9, we saw that the people overcame conspiracy through prayer and preparation.

When enemies are conspiring against your plan, the first thing you should do is fall on your knees and pray. Be prepared for a battle. Don't just hang loose, not read your Bible, panic, and throw in the towel!

Threats

The Bible tells you, "... *having done all, to stand*" (Ephesians 6:13). But some of us have tried to stand without first doing all. We don't read the Bible, pray and fast, or prepare ourselves in any way for what is a spiritual battle. Don't be a lazy Christian! Prayer and preparation are essential for you to overcome conspiracy, anger, and any other of the enemy's weapons, including the next weapon used by Sanballat — threats.

> *Then Judah said, "The strength of the laborers is failing, and there is so much rubbish that we are not able to build the wall." And our adversaries said, "They will neither know nor see anything, till we come into their midst and kill them and cause the work to cease." So it was, when the Jews who dwelt near them came, that they told us ten times, "From whatever place you turn, they will be upon us."* (NEHEMIAH 4:10-12)

Sanballat and his friends said, "Go ahead and work. But we're going to drop into the midst of everyone and just start killing the workers." That's quite a threat. How do you handle threats, especially threats against your life? Let me tell you what the Israelites did, as is recorded in the passage of Nehemiah 4:13–23.

> Many years ago, God opened a door for me to appear on the *Tom Snyder Show*, a midnight program that was aired nationally on NBC.

Certain workers were given swords, spears, and bows and were assigned to protect the others who continued working on the wall. Some fortified the wall while others built. Day and night, they were on guard against the enemy.

In the body of Christ, it takes some to pray, fast, and hang in there to watch over those who are out actively ministering. I know that it has given me great strength to have certain people say, "Marilyn, I really prayed and fasted for you during that time."

Overcoming the Enemy of Your Identity

Many years ago, God opened a door for me to appear on the *Tom Snyder Show*, a midnight program that was aired nationally on NBC. The program was to feature women who were evangelists. From watching the host, I gathered that he could really knock people down with his words. He just zeroed in on them and undid them in a very critical way. I thought, "What might he say to three women who are in full-time ministry?"

A whole group of people from my church set aside the day on which we taped the show, and they fasted and prayed all day. That night, they also came together and prayed. And do you know that the first question Tom Snyder asked was, "Can you tell me how to be born again?"

The enemy cannot win because Jesus is going to see that your identity is conformed to His.

For one solid hour, that program starred the Lord Jesus Christ. For one hour, no one was exalted but Jesus. Then, at the end, Tom said, "You know, I'd like to host programs like this four nights out of five each week. This was so much fun." Then he invited us to come back.

How did that wonderful experience come about? It happened because people were prepared with the weapons of spiritual warfare. They said, "We're building a wall for Jesus, and the devil cannot touch it." It takes constant preparation if you want to see your identity mature into the fullness of Jesus Christ.

How do you renew your mind? How is your identity conformed to God's? Simple! Stay in the Word, in church, and in prayer!

A certain woman in our church turned against my husband and me one time, and I felt very wounded. I wanted to call the woman and tell her off. Then I prayed, "Lord don't let me react with my reactions. Let me react with yours." In the end, I discovered that the woman was not really upset with my husband and me. Because she had been under tremendous pressure at home, she had taken it out on us. Instead of allowing me to tell her off, the Lord had led me to minister to this woman and encourage her in faith.

When threats and wounds come along, God has placed the body of Christ around us for fortification so that we might win over our trials. The walls of your identity will be built and the gates will be hung! The enemy cannot win because Jesus is going to see that your identity is conformed to His.

Paul reinforces this idea even further in Romans 12:2 when he tells us not to be conformed to this world: *"And do not be conformed to this world, but be transformed by the renewing of your mind, that you may prove what is that good and acceptable and perfect will of God."* How do you renew your mind? How is your identity conformed to God's? Simple! Stay in the Word, in church, and in prayer!

Dissension within the Ranks

Nehemiah and his people handled problems from the outside beautifully! But as soon as the last attack ended, an even worse one came along. Eventually, disunity broke out among the ranks. Can you imagine having to deal with quarrels after having been through those last attacks? They were too busy to waste time fighting with one another!

Nehemiah discovered that creditors who had lent money to the people who worked on the walls were charging exorbitant interest rates. Because of working on the wall, those in debt could not pay their bills. Therefore, they were losing property and everything they owned to their creditors.

Instead of allowing disunity to break up the ranks, as soon as Nehemiah heard about this oppression of the debtors, he admonished the creditors so that they could repent and come through in greater strength. Colossians 3:16 says, *"Let the word of Christ dwell in you richly in all wisdom, teaching and admonishing one another..."* It is interesting that it says, "Before you admonish, the Word of God has to dwell in you richly."

This is the ministry of helping our brothers to be mature, for admonish means "training by word, whether of encouragement, or, if necessary, by reproof or remonstrance." I like this definition from *Helps Word-studies*: "[Admonishment] exerts positive pressure on someone's logic ... urging them to choose ... God's best." It is a word full of hope!

Overcoming the Enemy of Your Identity

> *And we urge you, brethren, to recognize those who labor among you, and are over you in the Lord and admonish you, and to esteem them very highly in love for their work's sake. Be at peace among yourselves. Now we exhort you, brethren, warn those who are unruly, comfort the fainthearted, uphold the weak, be patient with all.* (1 THESSALONIANS 5:12-14)

Getting Sidetracked

God wants to help you overcome, not fail. He never sends people to condemn you and put you down. Often, you can perceive that the enemy is using someone simply because he condemns rather than convicts. I'm not saying that someone cannot point out a weak area to correct it. But he is not supposed to leave you dangling in defeat. The person who says, "Admit it, you've never done well," is dropping a package of hopelessness at your feet. That is not the voice of God; that is the voice of Sanballat.

Nehemiah overcame disharmony by lifting the people up out of the mess. But it was at this point in the story that the enemy began to get really crafty:

Now it happened when Sanballat, Tobiah, Geshem the Arab, and the rest of our enemies heard that I had rebuilt the wall, and that there were no breaks left in it (though at that time I had not hung the doors in the gates), that Sanballat and Geshem sent to me, saying, "Come, let us meet together among the villages in the plain of Ono." But they thought to do me harm. (NEHEMIAH 6:1-2)

Nehemiah received a message from his enemies that said, "Let's sit down and have a little friendly talk to straighten out the situation." But Nehemiah discerned their true purpose in writing to him, and here is how he answered:

So I sent messengers to them, saying, "I am doing a great work, so that I cannot come down. Why should the work cease while I leave it and go down to you?" But they sent me this message four times, and I answered them in the same manner. (NEHEMIAH 6:3-4)

Nehemiah received messages not once, but four times! And he said, "I answered the same way each time." You see, he overcame the devil's craftiness with wisdom and work. The devil wants to get you to quit. He'll say, "Stop working and get involved in a fight." Then you won't be out doing the Lord's work. When the devil tries to sidetrack you, don't even answer him. Don't give him the time of day. Just keep right on working and you won't be embroiled in a lot of garbage.

Treachery

The enemy's next trick was treachery. Sanballat sent a message to Nehemiah saying, "There is a prophet here who is prophesying against you." But the Lord helped Nehemiah to perceive the truth, and he did not listen to the false prophecy:

> *And I said, "Should such a man as I flee? And who is there such as I who would go into the temple to save his life? I will not go in!" Then I perceived that God had not sent him at all, but that he pronounced this prophecy against me because Tobiah and Sanballat had hired him. For this reason he was hired, that I should be afraid and act that way and sin, so that they might have cause for an evil report, that they might reproach me.*
>
> **(NEHEMIAH 6:11-13)**

The Holy Spirit will give you discernment when the enemy comes against you with words of fear. That's why we need to be led by the Spirit. Treachery is overcome by the discernment of God's voice.

Becoming an Overcomer

The enemy came with scorn and mockery, conspiracy, anger, threats, and disunity. He came with craftiness, accusations, and treachery. But Nehemiah never stopped working or said, "It's just too much. I give up." In every instance, the Holy Spirit caused

Overcoming the Enemy of Your Identity

Nehemiah to overcome the enemy. The Holy Spirit wants to make you an overcomer, too. Greater is He that is in you than he that is in the world (see 1 John 4:4). God does not want your identity or your life in a mess. He does not want you to be difficult or hard to get along with. He wants you to be an overcomer! He who is in you will overcome the forces of evil around you. Nehemiah won the victory, and it had quite an effect on the enemy:

> *And it happened, when all our enemies heard of it, and all the nations around us saw these things, that they were very disheartened in their own eyes; for they perceived that this work was done by our God.* (NEHEMIAH 6:16)

They knew that Nehemiah was doing God's work! How did they know? Because Nehemiah exercised prayer, self-control, bravery, and strength to fulfill his calling. All of those qualities were given to him by God, and God wants to pour those same qualities into you.

I want you to know that the enemy has already been overcome. His deeds were put down when Jesus went to the cross and then rose from the dead. The enemy's fate has been sealed and settled, and all you have to do is appropriate the victory that you have in Jesus. Today, Jesus wants you to enter into His victory and put down the enemy's works as you start becoming the complete person that was assigned to you at the new birth.

Chapter Five

God's Remedy for an Inferiority Complex

:::

One of the greatest needs in our lives today is the need to be free from an inferiority complex. All of us have areas in our lives where we feel inferior to other people. I heard a joke about a man who said, "I had an inferiority complex until I found out that I really was inferior." Actually, that joke loses its humor when you stop to think that too many people think they are inferior. Inferiority is one of the worst feelings a person can have!

I want you to look at a biblical example of a man who had one of the worst inferiority complexes I've ever seen. But God took this man, step-by-step, out of inferiority into achievement. God had to use this man to bring the nation of Israel out of a state of deep trouble that had come because of their refusal to serve God. In order for God to use this man as a deliverer, first he had to be delivered from the inferiority complex on his life.

God had warned the Israelites that if they served idols, the Canaanites and neighboring heathen tribes would become like "thorns" in Israel's side. God had said, "If you serve idols, you'll regret it," and Israel was regretting their idolatry because of the people of Midian.

The Midianites were a nation of cruel, abusive people whom God allowed to come against Israel. The people of Israel were so frightened that they were digging holes in the ground to live in or living in caves just to escape the Midianites.

The Israelites finally cried out, "God, help us!" Any person who cries out to God for help is going to receive help, but the Israelites' aid did not come exactly as they had planned. They thought that God was immediately going to send them a mighty deliverer. But God didn't send a deliverer at all, at least not in the beginning. He sent a prophet who came in and rebuked the people for their sin.

God's Remedy for an Inferiority Complex

The prophet told the people of Israel, "Until you correct your relationship with God, forget about changing the problems in your relationships with others. God led you out of Egypt with a mighty hand, and what have you done? You turned to serve the god of the Amorites, in whose land you dwell. You need to repent!" (see Judges 6:7–10.)

Nevertheless, God would send them a deliverer. He had already chosen a man who would deliver the nation of Israel from the Midianites. His name was Gideon.

The best way to get someone out of a negative complex is to start telling him what God's Word says.

From appearances, Gideon had everything going for him. His name means "feller" or "great warrior," in Hebrew, so he might have been a Mr. America in our day. He was the son of a man named Joash. You might say, "Gideon had what it took to be a leader!" But even with all of his positive attributes, Gideon had a serious inferiority complex.

When God sent an angel to Gideon, he was threshing wheat in a winepress to hide it from the Midianites. You can imagine his shock when, in the middle of such a desperate time, the angel spoke these encouraging words: *"The LORD is with you, you mighty man of valor!"* (Judges 6:12).

Gideon looked up and said, "Oh, really? Well, if the Lord is with us, why are the Midianites destroying Israel? Where are the miracles our fathers told us about? Where is God?"

God did not reproach Gideon for his questions. God didn't say, "Gideon, aren't you listening to me?" Instead, God gave Gideon another positive Scripture:

> *Then the LORD turned to him and said,*
> *"Go in this might of yours, and you shall*
> *save Israel from the hand of the Midianites.*
> *Have I not sent you?"* (JUDGES 6:14)

God was saying to Gideon, "If I am sending you, you won't fail. Don't worry about failure, Gideon." That's really positive. You see, Jesus did not intend for us to be inferior. He wants us to be superior. When the Lord sat down at the right hand of the Father, His work was finished. He had defeated the devil, hell, sin, the flesh, the world, and we are now seated in heavenly places with Him. God says, "If I'm with you, you'll have victory." Then Gideon told God, "How can I save Israel? My family is poor in Manasseh, and I am the least in my father's house." Don't believe that statement because it is a lie. You already know that Gideon's father was a town leader. Not only that, but Gideon himself had ten servants. How many of us have ten servants? Yet God wasn't choosing Gideon as a deliverer because of his status. Gideon, in spite of his inferiority complex, had a soft heart toward God. And God just kept giving Gideon more positive Scriptures: *"Surely I will be with you, and you shall defeat the Midianites as one man"* (Judges 6:16).

The best way to get someone out of a negative complex is to start telling him what God's Word says: *"He who is in you is greater than he who is in the world"* (1 John 4:4). And be of good cheer; you have overcome the world in Christ (John 16:33). God tells you who He is and reminds you that He is with you.

Gideon told the angel, "Since I have found grace in your sight, give me a sign that you have talked with me. Don't leave until I have made a sacrifice." Gideon brought a young goat, along with unleavened bread, and arranged them according to the angel's instruction. When it was ready, a fire came up out of the rock and consumed the sacrifice. God wanted Gideon to have a miracle to see that He was personally interested.

The next day, I went to Houston as planned. The Lord's powerful miracle of healing was such a personal statement of victory for me.

Sometimes we just need to see a miracle, don't we? I know of several times that God has allowed me to have miracles. He has made me use my own faith when I have felt chicken-hearted. For instance, once after a church service on a Sunday night, I came home feeling sick, sick, sick. I felt exhausted, and my stomach was uneasy.

The next morning, I had prayer, but that night I began feeling sick again. I started coughing, so my friends started praying some more. The next day, I felt no better, but I knew that I needed a miracle soon. I had to be in Houston in two days, so I needed a miracle of healing. The next morning, I felt sicker than ever. I was unable to get out of bed and was stumbling around from weakness when I tried to walk. I couldn't go to Houston; I couldn't leave my bed — I didn't even want to talk to anyone. I was still depending on my friends to have faith for my healing. Then the Lord began dealing with me, "I want you to have faith for yourself."

"I'm too sick. I don't even feel like praying. I want other people to believe for me." At that point, I was so hot that I took my temperature, which was 103 degrees. I thought, *I hope someone is praying, because I am really sick.* Then the Lord said, "What is wrong with your faith, Marilyn?"

"I don't have faith, Lord."

He said, "You do have faith." I looked at my thermometer again and rebuked the high fever. I said, "In 30 minutes I need to have a radical drop in my temperature. I demand it in Jesus's name." In 10 minutes, the fever had dropped to 102 degrees. In 20 minutes, it was 101 degrees, and in 30 minutes, it had dropped to 100 degrees! In the next hour, my husband came home, my temperature had become normal, and I was hungry again.

The next day, I went to Houston as planned. The Lord's powerful miracle of healing was such a personal statement of victory for me. It showed me how serious God is about wanting me to have faith, and it helped build my faith for future victories.

When Gideon saw the miracle of the fire consuming his sacrifice, he said, "I have seen God! I am going to die." Then in verse 23, the Lord spoke to Gideon, *"Peace be with you."* Did you know that Jesus wants you to have peace? He said, *"Peace I leave with you, My peace I give to you; not as the world gives do I give to you. Let not your heart be troubled, neither let it be afraid"* (John 14:27). Whatever God is doing in your life, He says, "Quit worrying! Take my peace."

Peace comes to you through Jesus. Peace doesn't just mean that you aren't fighting with someone; it means that you are living life at its highest. God was giving Gideon peace — the knowledge of life at its best — even before the battle started!

That day, Gideon saw God revealed as *Jehovah Shalom*, meaning, *"The-Lord-Is-Peace"* (Judges 6:24). Don't you think that was a beautiful day?

God's Remedy for an Inferiority Complex

Look at how God brought Gideon out of an inferiority complex. God told him who He was in God's eyes, He gave a visible miracle, and He gave Gideon peace.

After God did these things, you find that Gideon stopped asking so many questions and became much more cooperative. Still, God didn't lead Gideon out immediately into battle. Just as Gideon was led, step-by-step, out of an inferiority complex, he was also being led by God, step-by-step, into victory.

> *Now it came to pass the same night that the Lord said to him, "Take your father's young bull, the second bull of seven years old, and tear down the altar of Baal that your father has, and cut down the wooden image that is beside it."* (JUDGES 6:25)

After that, God had Gideon build an altar to the Lord and offer the second bull on it and use the wood from the image to offer the other bull. Gideon gathered his servants to help him carry out God's instructions. They did this at night because, frankly, Gideon didn't have the guts to do it by day.

But he didn't need to worry about being found out because God happens to be a tattletale, and God told on Gideon.

The next day, the men of Gideon's city arose early to go to their altar of Baal, but the altar was gone, and the image had been cut down. Instead of seeing an altar to Baal, the men saw an altar to Jehovah God upon which a young bull had been sacrificed. Then the men began to ask, "Who did this?" Another man spoke up, "It was Gideon, the son of Joash." God didn't let Gideon off the hook. He was found out anyway.

> **God is very patient to help people who have inferiority complexes. He wants so much to build a sense of confidence and security in them.**

The men said, "Gideon has insulted Baal, so we have to kill him." Joash defended his son and told the men that if Baal was a god, he could defend himself. At this point in the story, Gideon must have suddenly become fired up. He became the "muscle man" that his name indicated. Joash said, "Come on! Isn't Baal big enough to fight his own battles? If Baal is mad at Gideon, let him fight him!"

The men who worshiped Baal thought, *That's fair enough.* His father then called Gideon "Jerubbaal," which means *"Let Baal contend against him"* (Judges 6:32 NASB). These names are so important in helping us understand the full meaning of what happened. Later in 2 Samuel 11:21, Gideon is called "Jerubbesheth," which means "shame will contend." In this case the idol is shame, "shame (i.e. the idol) will contend." Since Baal never took revenge on Gideon, God put Baal to shame.

After his father had renamed Gideon, the Midianites arrived in town. But they didn't come alone; they brought the Amalekites with them. Can you imagine Gideon's looking on and wondering, *God, where are you?* But God was ready to help Gideon face his enemies, so the next thing He did was make Gideon a charismatic: *"But the Spirit of the LORD came upon Gideon; then he blew the trumpet, and the Abiezrites gathered behind him"* (Judges 6:34).

This is very interesting in the Hebrew translation. The words "came upon" basically mean that Gideon was clothed from his head to his toes in the Spirit of God. Isn't that great? Gideon's identity may have been full of holes, but God took care of those holes by clothing Gideon in the Spirit. But even after the Spirit came upon Gideon, he still had some problems with reverting back to his old inferiority complex. Soon he began thinking, *I wonder if this is really God calling me?*

You may think, *This is quite a problem with Gideon!* But God wants to show us the worst case to prove that He can cure all of us from inferiority.

Wanting to be sure about the Lord's call, Gideon said, "I am going to lay a fleece outside on the ground. In the morning, if the fleece is wet but the ground around it is dry, I'll know that this is God." God answered Gideon's fleece. Then Gideon said, "God, don't be mad, but I want to make sure one more time. This time let the fleece be dry and the ground all wet."

God answered Gideon's fleece again. I thought, *Oh, God, you are so patient.* God is very patient to help people who have inferiority complexes. He wants so much to build a sense of confidence and security in them.

God's Remedy for an Inferiority Complex

Once, in dealing with my son, I learned something about people with inferiority complexes. It proved how careful we must be to not build inferiority complexes in others. I asked my son, "Haven't you finished mowing the lawn yet?"

He said, "No, I'm just lazy."

I told him, "Don't ever say that about yourself! That is a terrible thing to say."

"Well, you say it."

I never again said that my son was lazy. We need to build patiently and not destroy, just as God patiently built confidence in Gideon's life.

At the same time that God was building Gideon up, everybody else was calling Gideon "Jerubbaal," or "Let Baal contend with him." Imagine everybody calling you that, rather than your real name. How could you not feel better about yourself? How do you think Gideon felt?

When Gideon found out that the enemies had come in, he rallied the people together, and 32,000 people showed up. That sounds like enough people to do the job, doesn't it? But then God told Gideon, "These are just too many people. If all these people win the battle, they will take the credit instead of giving it to me. Send every fearful person home."

God's advice was, of course, very scriptural because the book of Deuteronomy says that if a man had just taken a wife, planted a crop, or was afraid, he could go home from battle. Gideon said, "Everyone who is afraid can go home," and 22,000 people left. Gideon wasn't the only one with an inferiority complex, was he?

> When God's Word hits our earthen vessels, it creates more than a hairline crack. It breaks us so that Jesus's light can come shining through.

Gideon was probably wondering, "How will we fight a battle with only 10,000 people?" But God spoke up, "There are still too many people."

"What are you trying to do, God? Kill me?"

God said, "Lead the people to the water and let them drink. Those who put their whole faces in the water to drink have to go home, but those who cup the water in their hand will stay for the battle."

God's Remedy for an Inferiority Complex

Gideon brought the people to the water, and 9,700 of the men put their faces in the water to drink. Now Gideon had 300 men. By this time, Gideon may have been thinking of surrender. But that night, as he prepared to take his rest before the battle, God said, "Gideon, if you are still afraid, I want you to do something else."

What do you mean, "If Gideon is still afraid?" Of course, he was afraid, knowing that he and only 300 men would face the Midianites and the Amalekites! God said, "Take your servant and go listen to the camp of the Midianites and Amalekites as they are talking in their camp."

Gideon and his servant sneaked down to the Midianite tents, and as they approached the camp, they heard two men talking. Here is the conversation that Gideon overheard:

> "I have had a dream: To my surprise, a loaf of barley bread tumbled into the camp of Midian; it came to a tent and struck it so that it fell and overturned, and the tent collapsed." Then his companion answered and said, "This is nothing else but the sword of Gideon

the son of Joash, a man of Israel! Into his hand God has delivered Midian and the whole camp." (JUDGES 7:13-14)

Who caused the Midianite man to dream this dream? It was God, the tattletale! Isn't it strange that the man dreamed of a barley loaf? God was saying to Gideon, "You and your men are far more than just a little piece of bread or a few crumbs. You are a whole barley loaf! Some people might think you're an oaf, but you're a loaf!"

The man's confession of his dream deeply touched Gideon, and the Bible tells us that upon hearing the interpretation, Gideon "worshiped the Lord." Gideon returned to the Israelite army and said, *"Arise, for the LORD has delivered the camp of Midian into your hand"* (Judges 7:15).

The men of Israel were divided into three companies, and every man had a trumpet and an empty pitcher with a lamp in it. Gideon said, "When we come to the outside of the enemy camp, do exactly what I do. When I blow my trumpet, I want you to blow your trumpets and shout, *'The sword of the LORD, and of Gideon!'"* (v. 18)

God's Remedy for an Inferiority Complex

I thought, *Gideon, you aren't the timid little thing you used to be. You're even putting your name in there!* Gideon knew who he was because God had healed him from an inferiority complex. Step-by-step, Gideon was delivered and showed his ability in God.

After reaching the Midianite camp, all the men followed Gideon's actions, blowing their trumpets and shouting, "The sword of the Lord, and of Gideon!" Then each man struck his pitcher, and when the pitchers broke, the lamps were struck by the cold night air, and each one lit up.

Aren't we the same way? The Bible calls us "earthen vessels," and it calls God's Word a "two-edged sword that divides soul from spirit." When God's Word hits our earthen vessels, it creates more than a hairline crack. It breaks us so that Jesus's light can come shining through.

The Israelites' light began to shine, and confusion broke out in the ranks of the Midianites. Imagine their confusion when, all of a sudden, they heard hundreds of trumpets, pitchers shattering, and men shouting, and saw light shining all around? Instead of running for help from the Amalekites, the Midianites began fighting with the Amalekites, and they began killing each other! The Israelites then chased after the Midianites and Amalekites, and as they did so, they called for additional men to fortify the ranks. Gideon called to the men from the tribe of Ephraim, "Come down quickly!" The men from the tribes of Ephraim, Naphtali, Manasseh, and Asher all came to help, and they all started killing Midianites right and left.

I see in Gideon a truly Spirit-led, Spirit-filled identity. But it took God's dealing for Gideon to reach that place of security.

In this part of the battle, the tribe of Ephraim is especially recognized for slaying two Midianite princes, Oreb and Zeeb. But these victories don't end the story. In the end, you see Gideon as a different man than the easily intimidated man he had been when he was first called by God.

In Judges chapter eight, the men of Ephraim asked Gideon, "Why didn't you call us to fight in the beginning?"

God's Remedy for an Inferiority Complex

If I had been Gideon, my natural response would have been, "Look, guys, I called 32,000 men from my own tribe, but 22,000 of them went home because they were afraid. Then God told me to send home everyone who lapped the water like a dog, and that was another 9,700 of them. I only had 300 men to fight! If you don't like the way I handled it, talk to God. He's the one who gave me directions."

We can really be defensive — especially with relatives. Ephraim had been Manasseh's brother, so both tribes were originally sons of Jacob. Nobody can get under your skin more effectively than a relative — but the men of Ephraim didn't bother Gideon at all! In fact, he had a beautiful reaction:

> *So he said to them, "What have I done now in comparison with you? Is not the gleaning of the grapes of Ephraim better than the vintage of Abiezer? God has delivered into your hands the princes of Midian, Oreb and Zeeb. And what was I able to do in comparison with you?" Then their anger toward him subsided when he said that.* (JUDGES 8:2-3)

First, Gideon esteemed the tribe of Ephraim above his own tribe. And in his comparison, Gideon didn't even mention his own name, but instead he spoke of Abiezer, his ancestor. Then Gideon said, "You're far better than I am, because you killed the princes of Midian! Nothing I've done compares to that." Gideon had become so secure about his ability in God that he didn't have to be defensive. It was more important to him to keep peace with his brothers.

Years later, Solomon, in his wisdom, wrote, "*A soft answer turns away wrath*" (Proverbs 15:1). In the example of Gideon, his soft answer and unwillingness to quarrel turned away the anger and contention of the men of Ephraim. I see in Gideon a truly Spirit-led, Spirit-filled identity. But it took God's dealing for Gideon to reach that place of security.

How was he delivered by God from an inferiority complex? God lifted him with the Word, filled him with His Holy Spirit, showed him several miracles, gave him peace, and brought victory. That is exciting. But even more exciting, if you look to God for these same things, He will do for you what He did for Gideon.

Chapter Six

Dedicating Your Identity to God

∷

God wants us to have complete identities, but then He also wants our identities to be dedicated to Him. The twelfth chapter of Nehemiah shows all of God's people gathering together to dedicate the walls and gates to Him. It wasn't just a few people coming together for a small dedication. Singers, musicians, princes, farmers, and merchants from all over the land came to dedicate the walls to God.

Dedication was not a dry, dull occasion. It brought the people great joy:

> *Now at the dedication of the wall of Jerusalem they sought out the Levites in all their places, to bring them to Jerusalem to*

> *celebrate the dedication with gladness, both with thanksgivings and singing, with cymbals and stringed instruments and harps. . . . That day they offered great sacrifices, and rejoiced, for God had made them rejoice with great joy; the women and the children also rejoiced, so that the joy of Jerusalem was heard afar off.*
>
> (NEHEMIAH 12:27, 43)

When you dedicate your identity to God, it will make you rejoice. Other people will notice it, just as the people from "afar off" noticed the joy of God's people on this day of dedication. People will see you and say, "Why are they so happy? I wish I could be that happy."

It is very important that every day we say, "God, I dedicate my identity and my reactions to you. I want you to react through me today." If you do not dedicate your identity and your reactions, then the devil can steal back some of the territory that you have gained.

When you begin to lose your temper, feel offended, or get depressed, then you need to pray quickly, "God, my identity is yours." Then your identity won't end

Dedicating Your Identity to God

up in defeat. You will be acting like God, and God always wins.

I want to look back at a story from the book of 2 Samuel. This is a story that contrasts two identities: that of King David and his counselor, Ahithophel. King David's mistakes stand out as having been far worse than any of Ahithophel's mistakes, yet King David still ended up as a winner. Ahithophel, however, ended up in death and defeat because he did not close the gates of his identity to the enemy.

I know how fathers feel about their daughters; but if ever a girl is adored, it is by her grandfather!

Ahithophel's name means "brother of folly," but in the beginning of his life he did not look like a man of folly. He looked like a very brilliant man who was a counselor to the king of Israel. King David loved, admired, and respected this man very deeply. I wondered, *How could a man like Ahithophel end up being a traitor?* I looked more closely at his family and circumstances and came to some very interesting conclusions.

I found out that Ahithophel was the grandfather of a woman named Bathsheba. I know how fathers feel about their daughters; but if ever a girl is adored, it is by her grandfather! Bathsheba was probably raised well, and her parents must have been very selective in choosing her husband. Her husband Uriah turned out to be such a dedicated and ardent Jew that any father would have been proud to have him as a son-in-law.

Until this time, Ahithophel had not been aware of David's involvement with Bathsheba.

One evening, David looked outside his palace from a rooftop and saw Bathsheba bathing nearby. The Bible tells you that this incident happened at a time when kings went to war. The rest of Israel's men were at war, and that is where David should have been. But because he was spending time in idleness, he ended up sending for Bathsheba and committing adultery with her. It was not long afterward that David discovered Bathsheba was pregnant with his child.

David immediately sent for Bathsheba's husband, Uriah. If Uriah went home and slept with Bathsheba, he would think that she was expecting his child. But when Uriah came home, he was so devoted to his duty at war that he refused to go home to his wife. He said:

> *"The ark and Israel and Judah are dwelling in tents, and my lord Joab and the servants of my lord are encamped in the open fields. Shall I then go to my house to eat and drink, and to lie with my wife? As you live, and as your soul lives, I will not do this thing."* (2 SAMUEL 11:11)

If anything ever made David feel guilty, it was Uriah's words. David sent Uriah back to battle and ordered him to fight in the front lines so that he would be killed. Now David was guilty of murder as well as adultery.

After Uriah's death, the Lord sent a prophet named Nathan to David. "You are really going to suffer for your sin. And Bathsheba's child is going to die."

Until this time, Ahithophel had not been aware of David's involvement with Bathsheba. But when Nathan's prophecy exposed the truth, I think it must have deeply hurt Ahithophel. I am sure that bitterness took root and began to grow in his heart. Yet he walked carefully before King David and never provoked him in any way. As Ahithophel walked, I believe he was waiting for an opportunity to take revenge for the honor of his granddaughter.

Apparently, Ahithophel found his opportunity in turning his support away from David to David's son, Absalom. Absalom was a handsome, brilliant young man who made David very proud. The Bible says that from the sole of his foot to the crown of his head, Absalom did not have one blemish (2 Samuel 14:25).

David had no idea that his authority as king was being usurped by his own son.

He had so much hair that every year when it was cut off, the cut hair weighed about five pounds. You talk about women being vain — I think that's the height of vanity! I thought, *God, why did you waste all that wonderful hair on a man?*

Despite the fact that Absalom killed his brother Amnon because he had raped his sister, Tamar, and then fled to Geshur, David adored his son. Apparently, the feeling was not mutual. Even after his return to Israel, Absalom was so full of anger and pride that eventually he decided he would make a better king than his father. Second Samuel 15 tells you that Absalom would sit by the gates of the city and win the hearts of the people to himself:

> *Then Absalom would say to him, "Look, your case is good and right; but there is no deputy of the king to hear you." Moreover Absalom would say, "Oh, that I were made judge in the land, and everyone who has any suit or cause would come to me; then I would give him justice."* (2 SAMUEL 15:3-4)

As the townspeople passed by the city gate, Absalom talked to them and said, "My father doesn't really care about what's going on. He's out of touch, but I'm not. If I were the king, I would help you." The Bible tells us that Absalom "stole the hearts" of the people of Israel. David had no idea that his authority as king was being usurped by his own son, but I can guarantee you that Ahithophel was very aware of what was happening.

One day, Absalom finally pronounced himself king, and the kingdom of Israel was divided in its loyalties. Half of the kingdom still favored their former king, David. But the rest of the people's hearts were with Absalom. As soon as Absalom announced his kingship, David had to flee from the city to protect his life. And as soon as David fled, Ahithophel was at Absalom's side offering counsel.

Absalom preferred Hushai's counsel to that of Ahithophel and decided to wait before pursuing David.

Absalom's other counselor was a man named Hushai, who still favored David secretly. He was with Absalom, but he was pretending to be loyal in order to protect David. When Absalom asked Ahithophel how David should be dealt with, Ahithophel said, "Let me choose 12,000 men. We will pursue David and all his people." Then Ahithophel added, *"I will strike only the king"* (2 Samuel 17:2).

When I read this, I think, *Ahithophel, you're really in a hurry to kill David!*

Dedicating Your Identity to God

Why would the king's own counselor want to murder the man for whom he worked? Because the thought had been brewing in his heart for years. Now Ahithophel's big opportunity for revenge had come, and when he spoke, it was, "Murder, murder, murder."

But Absalom was not content simply to take Ahithophel's advice without getting a second opinion. He asked Hushai his opinion, and Hushai said, "Don't go tonight because David's men are angry and upset. They will be ready for blood."

Absalom preferred Hushai's counsel to that of Ahithophel and decided to wait before pursuing David. But the rejection of his own counsel was more than Ahithophel could bear. The Bible tells you that in his sorrow over having his counsel rejected, Ahithophel rode to his home and committed suicide by hanging himself.

This is not the end of the story. In the search for David, Absalom went out with his army of men. As he rode along, his beautiful hair was caught in the branches of a tree. The donkey rode out from under Absalom and left him hanging still alive between heaven and earth. David had instructed his men, "Don't kill Absalom, whatever you do." But Joab, the leader of David's army, killed Absalom, despite David's instructions to spare Absalom's life. I think he realized the threat that he would still present to David's reign. After Absalom was murdered, the news was brought to David, and it grieved him deeply. There was no malice in the words he spoke: "*O my son Absalom — my son, my son Absalom — if only I had died in your place! O Absalom my son, my son!*" (2 Samuel 18:33).

Guard Your Gates Against the Enemy

I looked at David's character and saw no bitterness toward the son who had wanted to kill his own father. I saw no bitterness in David toward Ahithophel, who had been vengeful and a traitor. David had once been responsible for adultery and the murder of Bathsheba's husband. Ahithophel, as far as I know, never did either. But he ended up committing suicide. David, the ex-adulterer and ex-murderer, was taken back across the Jordan and was restored as Israel's king.

Dedicating Your Identity to God

I would say that David's identity seemed to fail more times than Ahithophel's identity. But Ahithophel did not guard his gates against the enemy. He let bitterness, hatred, and revenge come in. The gates of his identity were closed to God, but they were open to the enemy's plans of dissension. Because of these things, Ahithophel died a broken man, while David came back as a winner.

Ahithophel could have called on God and repented that night when he gave bad counsel to Absalom.

David was willing to expose his identity to God, even when he was wrong. When Nathan prophesied to David, "There is sin in your life," David said, "That is exactly right. I'm a sinner. I'm an adulterer and a murderer." The Bible says that the person who covers his sin will not prosper (Proverbs 28:13). But the person who repents of sin brings in God's forgiveness and cleansing. True, David made mistakes, but he was repentant — a man after God's own heart. He kept his identity dedicated to God, regardless of his mistakes along the way.

I believe David wrote Psalm 55 as an outpouring of his heart because of Ahithophel's betrayal:

> *For it is not an enemy who reproaches me;*
> *Then I could bear it.*
> *Nor is it one who hates me who has*
> *　　exalted himself against me;*
> *Then I could hide from him.*
> *But it was you, a man my equal,*
> *My companion and my acquaintance.*
> *We took sweet counsel together,*
> *And walked to the house of God in the throng.*
> *Let death seize them;*
> *Let them go down alive into hell,*
> *For wickedness is in their dwellings*
> *　　and among them.*
> *As for me, I will call upon God,*
> *And the* LORD *shall save me.* (PSALM 55:12-16)

Ahithophel could have called on God and repented that night when he gave bad counsel to Absalom. He could have confessed his sin to God and not ended up committing suicide. Through all the ages, Ahithophel is not remembered as being a wise man but is known as having been defeated because he allowed the gates of his identity to be broken down by the enemy.

Oh, the importance of dedicating our identities daily to God so that bitterness may not enter our lives!

You might say, "He had a right to be bitter." As Christians, we have no right to be bitter. We have no right to hate. The only right we have is that of allowing Jesus Christ to react through us. I thought, *Ahithophel, what a shame that you ended up as a brother of folly, just like the meaning of your name!*

David's openness was so pleasing to God that He said, "David, your throne will never end." And David ended up in the lineage of our Lord Jesus Christ.

Oh, the importance of dedicating our identities daily to God so that bitterness may not enter our lives! David dedicated his identity to God, and it was worth it. You can be a king, or you can be a spiritual suicide. Which will you choose? Choose to be a king and a priest!

Create in me a clean heart, O God,
And renew a steadfast spirit within me.
Do not cast me away from Your presence,
And do not take Your Holy Spirit from me.

Restore to me the joy of Your salvation,
And uphold me by Your generous Spirit.

(PSALM 51:10-12)

(A Psalm of David when Nathan the prophet went to him, after he had gone in to Bathsheba.)

Chapter Seven

God Can Stabilize an Unstable Identity

∴

Have you ever known Christians who had a specific call of God on their lives yet were up one minute and down the next? All of us have a specific call, whether or not it is in the full-time ministry. And just as all of us are called to a divine plan, we are also familiar with the frustration that Paul described in Romans 7:15, "*For what I am doing, I do not understand. For what I will to do, that I do not practice; but what I hate, that I do.*"

Have you ever done something that you just hated — yet you did it anyway? Those are areas of instability in our lives where God wants to perform a transformation. I want you to see how God took a person who, as far as appearances were concerned, blew it in every way God had for him. We might look at such a person today and say, "Wow, he really needs counseling. He has big problems!"

In studying the life of Samson, you will see how, even though he had a marvelous call of God on his life, he made some big mistakes. Yet God redeemed Samson's unstable identity in the end, just as God wants to redeem unstable areas in our own identities.

Judges 13 tells us that an angel came to a woman from the tribe of Dan and brought her a wonderful message: *"Indeed now, you are barren and have borne no children, but you shall conceive and bear a son"* (v. 3).

As the woman listened to the angel's message, she was told, "You are not to drink wine or strong drink or touch any unclean thing. From the time he is conceived in your womb, he will be a Nazarite unto God."

According to Numbers 6:1–21, the Nazarite vow was for people to set themselves apart to God for certain periods of time, usually 60 to 90 days. During that time, the person would not drink anything of an alcoholic nature, touch anything unclean, or cut their hair.

God Can Stabilize an Unstable Identity

Basically, the angel sent to the woman of the tribe of Dan was saying that her son was to be set apart with God's call on his life from the moment of conception. He was to observe the Nazarite vow not for 60 or 90 days but for the span of his entire life. In order for Samson to have been separated to God from the time of conception, his mother had to observe the Nazarite vow from the moment she received the angel's message to the time of Samson's birth.

This was a very difficult and trying time for Israel, so the angelic prophecy of a deliverer was exciting news!

At this point in time, Israel was being overwhelmed and oppressed by the Philistine nation, a people who were from the Mediterranean coast of southern Israel. The Philistines were a very strong and aggressive nation who infiltrated the tribes of Israel and slowly overcame them. The Israelites were squelched by this new Philistine government, which was very authoritarian. The people of Israel were not even allowed to have any metal with which to make weapons. The few knives given to the Israelites had to be sharpened under Philistine supervision. There were no swords, and even ordinary work tools were monitored. This was a very difficult and trying time for Israel, so the angelic prophecy of a deliverer was exciting news!

Upon hearing the angel's message from the Lord, the woman became very excited. The Bible doesn't tell her age, but I have a feeling that she was middle-aged and was previously unable to bear children. She ran to tell her husband about the angelic visitation, and he had a really great response:

> *Then Manoah prayed to the* Lord, *and said, "O my Lord, please let the Man of God whom You sent come to us again and teach us what we shall do for the child who will be born."*
> (JUDGES 13:8)

The father-to-be, Manoah, said, "We need to know how to raise this special child!" He was really excited, because the angel had promised that this child would be a deliverer of Israel from the Philistines.

God answered Manoah's prayer and sent the angel a second time to emphasize the Nazarite vow.

God Can Stabilize an Unstable Identity

Manoah prepared an offering, and the angel wondrously ascended in the flame of fire.

When the child was born, the woman chose Samson for his name. Samson means "sunlight," because this child would bring light into a very dark situation. Not only was his important birth prophesied to his parents by an angel, but it was also prophesied in Genesis chapter 49. Jacob prophesied over his son, Dan, and spoke of one who would "judge his people." According to the Old Testament, the only judge who came from the tribe of Dan was Samson. As you can see, he was a very important part of Israel's destiny.

After Samson's birth, the Lord blessed him. In Judges 14:6 and 19, it says that the Spirit of the Lord came upon him. The Hebrew wording for the Spirit coming upon Samson is very unusual. It is not the same thing as when we say, "The Lord moved upon my heart to do this." Rather, the Spirit of the Lord "rushed upon Samson and made him successful" with a special anointing of strength. Why an anointing of strength? Because God was calling Samson to be a one-man army for Israel!

So far, you've seen the positive characteristics of Samson's identity, but he had negative ones, too. For one thing, Samson liked the wrong kind of women. The Bible tells you about three women to whom he was attracted, and they were all Philistines. That in itself was bad news for someone with a calling like Samson's! It's just like the devil to dress up sin in an attractive package to lure people from their callings. The Philistines were an evil people, and Samson was supposed to deliver his people from them — not get involved with their women! But as soon as the Bible tells you about Samson's anointings, it also reveals his weaknesses.

An anointing from God is not just so you can carry out His plans for your life. It is also given to cover weaknesses in your identity . . .

It is always a shock to see a person who is very anointed of God having strong identity problems. Samson's first major mistake came in Judges 14:1 when he *"saw a woman in Timnah of the daughters of the Philistines."* Samson immediately fell in love and decided to marry the woman. But when he told his parents about his decision, of course, they were very

God Can Stabilize an Unstable Identity

distraught. You say, "Why wouldn't they be upset when their son wants to marry the daughter of an enemy tribe?" Yet interestingly enough, Judges 14:4 tells us, *"But his father and mother did not know that it was of the* Lord *— that he was seeking an occasion to move against the Philistines."* God could use even this situation for His glory.

Having told his parents about his love for the Philistine woman, Samson and his parents headed off for Timnah. On his way, a tremendous anointing of strength came upon Samson when a lion came roaring out against him. The Spirit came upon Samson, and he ripped the lion apart as though it were a little goat. You see, Samson was entering Philistine territory, and he needed to know that God was giving him an anointing to take him through.

An anointing from God is not just so you can carry out His plans for your life. It is also given to cover weaknesses in your identity so that you can be strong in Him. God wanted Samson to be strong in his identity when he encountered the Philistine people.

Samson's marriage feast was arranged in Timnah, and then you see a second weakness pop up in his identity: his love for practical jokes and riddles, which Samson never seemed to outgrow. At his wedding feast, he told a riddle and said, "Anyone who knows the answer will receive 30 linen garments and 30 changes of clothes."

Maybe Samson figured out that if he didn't get clothes as wedding gifts, he could get them through making this bet with the other men. Maybe he just wanted new clothes for his honeymoon. Whatever the case, Samson was sure that nobody would guess this riddle: *"Out of the eater came something to eat, and out of the strong came something sweet"* (Judges 14:14).

Seven days passed, and nobody could guess the answer to Samson's riddle. Samson wasn't the Philistines' favorite person anyway because he was an Israelite. But it infuriated the men that they could not guess his riddle. Finally, they approached his wife with threats: "If you don't find out the answer, we'll burn your parents' house." She was so fearful that she began using every possible means to pry the answer to the riddle from Samson. "Oh, Samson, if you love me, you will tell me the answer."

Samson finally gave his wife the riddle answer: *"What is sweeter than honey? And what is stronger than a lion?"* (Judges 14:18). The girl then told it to her

God Can Stabilize an Unstable Identity

people, and when the men brought the answer to Samson, he was furious! At that moment, the Spirit of the Lord came upon him mightily. In a burst of anointed strength, Samson went to Ashkelon, slew 30 men, stole their clothing, and gave it to the men who had guessed the riddle.

Sometime later, during the wheat harvest, Samson returned to Timnah and to his wife, only to learn that the Philistines had given her away to his best man. The girl's father said, "Sorry, but I already gave her away in marriage. Take her younger sister instead."

This is where Samson really became upset. Remember, it was his nature to play pranks. The next thing he did was to take 300 foxes and tie their tails together with torches in between, two by two. Then he sent the foxes into some Philistine wheat fields and burned them to the ground.

Can you imagine just catching those foxes and tying their tails together? Why not just set fire to the wheat fields? Because a true prankster would be more creative! But the sad part of this story was the revenge. The Philistines went to the home of Samson's would-be wife and killed her and her father, burning them to death. She had moved against Samson in fear for her life, but eventually she was killed anyway. Now Samson had a great thirst for vengeance, and he attacked and killed many Philistines before moving to a place called Etam.

While Samson was living in Etam, the Philistines, knowing the fear they invoked in the people of Israel, went to Samson's people and asked where he was so they could exact revenge. The Israelites didn't back Samson at all. Instead, 3,000 men of Judah went after Samson and said, "We came to bind you up so that we can deliver you to the Philistines." Samson allowed them to bind him up, provided they didn't kill him. When the Philistines saw him, they thought, *We've got him now.* They were ready to kill him. But the Bible says that at that moment, the Spirit of the Lord came mightily upon Samson, and he threw off the cords as though they were nothing. Then he found the jawbone of a donkey, with which he killed 1,000 Philistine men.

I partially blame Israel for Samson's inability to handle his weaknesses. Remember that, outside of his parents' support, Samson stood alone. Never do you see Israel standing supportively behind him. In

God Can Stabilize an Unstable Identity

fact, the moment threats came to them, they delivered Samson to the enemy themselves!

How many times has God called a person and anointed him, yet been unable to find a person willing to pray for him? For example, instead of backing a pastor, the congregation binds him by picking him to pieces with criticism. Israel saw Samson's weaknesses, as well as his strengths, but didn't back him either. The only thing the Israelites cared about was how they could benefit in any situation.

You would think that after such mischief, Samson might have been smart enough not to get too closely involved with the Philistines.

For 20 years, Samson judged Israel consistently. He was a good judge, and the Bible says nothing negative about how he handled the job. But he still wasn't immune from temptation. Sometimes, if things aren't really exciting, or they're too much the same, we can get bored. The enemy comes along and says, "Take a spiritual vacation. Live it up and nobody will know."

Samson still had a yearning for a Philistine woman — the wrong kind of woman. The weakness hadn't been corrected. Samson had not dealt with his weaknesses, but he had not lost the anointing of God, either.

One day, Samson went to a place called Gaza and became involved with a harlot. When the Philistines found out about Samson's involvement with this harlot, they really harassed him about it. Finally, Samson had taken his fill of harassment, so he decided that it was time for another practical joke. This time he arose early one morning, went to Gaza's main entrance, pulled off the entire huge gate and set it up on a hill, for spite. Here it was — 20 years later, and Samson was still pulling pranks!

The next morning, when the Philistines found that the city gate had been placed up on a hill, they didn't have to ask who had done it. They knew that Samson had been the culprit.

You would think that after such mischief, Samson might have been smart enough not to get too closely involved with the Philistines. But immediately, he went again into Philistine territory, and this time he became involved with another woman. This woman

God Can Stabilize an Unstable Identity

was well-described in Proverbs 6:26, which says, *"The adulteress will hunt for the precious life"* (KJV). An adulteress isn't just selling her body for a piece of bread or a new dress. She is a woman with a plot and is after everything that a man owns.

This is a picture of a woman whose name was Delilah, and her name means "feeble, delicate." You know, the type who says, "I can't do anything on my own . . . I'm just so helpless." But she wasn't dependent at all! She was a sly one.

As soon as the Philistine men discovered that Samson was seeing Delilah, they came to Delilah and said, "Each of us will give you 1,100 pieces of silver if you find out the secret of Samson's strength." That was a lot of money to Delilah, and she was not in love with Samson. She was in love with money. Delilah knew that Samson was physically attracted to her, and she used that attraction as her weapon against him. One day she said, "Oh, Samson, I wish you would tell me what makes you so strong."

He said, "Well, if you bind me with brand new bowstrings, that will do it." So, one night, Delilah put Samson to sleep, bound him, and then yelled, "Samson, the Philistines are upon you!" Samson awakened instantly, breaking out of the ropes with ease. When he realized what Delilah had done, he laughed. After all, he was a prankster who loved a good joke.

Samson would only tease Delilah about the secret of his strength. Once, he told her that if she bound him with new ropes, he would be as weak as other men. That night, Delilah bound Samson with new ropes as he slept and then cried, "The Philistines be upon you, Samson!" Before the "Philistines" could take Samson, he broke the cords "like a thread."

To repent means to "turn back," so Samson was turning toward God again. His anointing was coming back.

Delilah made up her mind, "I have to be more feeble and more delicate," and she set herself to the task. "Samson, you really don't love me, or you would tell me the secret of your strength." She vexed him every day: "You just make fun of me, but you won't tell me the truth." The Bible says that finally, Samson's soul was "vexed to death," and he told Delilah the truth. He said, "I have been a Nazarite unto God from my mother's womb. If I am shaven, then my strength will go from me."

That night, Delilah put Samson to sleep on her knees and called for a man who was waiting nearby with a razor. The seven locks of Samson's hair were shaven from his head, and then Delilah began to afflict Samson, "The Philistines are upon you!" When Samson arose, he did not realize that his anointing of strength was gone. The Philistine men took him away immediately and put out his eyes. He was taken to Gaza. I thought, *Samson, your wandering eyes caused you to sin, and now they have been put out. You played cruel jokes in Gaza, and now you have become the joke.*

Samson was bound with fetters of brass and was made to work grinding grain in a prison house — a woman's work. While he was grinding, his hair slowly began to grow. But Samson's hair wasn't the only thing that was changing. His heart was also changing in repentance. To repent means to "turn back," so Samson was turning toward God again. His anointing was coming back.

One day, the Philistines held a great feast for Dagon, their idol. Everybody became very drunk, so they called for Samson, to make a big joke of him.

Some little boy led Samson out, since Samson could not see. Samson told the little boy to lead him to the space between the two pillars. The two pillars were the supports for the entire house in which the Philistines sat. All the major men of leadership were present on that day.

Once he had taken his place, Samson prayed a beautiful prayer that showed his total identity turn-around:

> "Then Samson called to the LORD, saying,
> "O LORD God, remember me, I pray!
> Strengthen me, I pray, just this once, O God,
> that I may with one blow take vengeance on
> the Philistines for my two eyes!" (JUDGES 16:28)

When Samson said, "O LORD God," he used God's name, *Adonai*, which means "Master." Then in that same statement he used the word *Yahweh*, which is the name God uses for Himself when relating to His chosen people in the Old Testament. Finally, when Samson said, "Oh God," he was using God's name, *Elohim*. The Lord God. He is the "supreme God," our "creator," and the "mighty one."

God Can Stabilize an Unstable Identity

For the most part, Samson had known God the way most Christians know Him: as *Elohim*, and one who gives strength. Samson also knew God as *Jehovah*, the one who reveals His Holy Spirit and His identity to man. But Samson had never before made God his master and owner. Never before had Samson said, "God, you call the shots. I will obey." Samson had always called his own shots, but on this day, he called him "Lord."

Let's remember that after our identities have been dedicated to God, He wants to stay the Master over our weaknesses.

We can be filled with the Spirit, but if we don't allow God to be more than our Savior, our identities will stay in defeat. He is the one to whom we must submit our identities. You don't have to hate your actions — the weak areas of your identity — that betray your heart. You just have to know God as *Adonai* or "Master."

Samson said, "Oh, God, let me be avenged of the Philistines." Not, "God, I'll do it," but "God, you do it." Samson was fulfilling his call in God's way. He grasped the two pillars, between which he stood, and prayed, "Let me die with the Philistines." Samson pushed with an anointing of strength on those pillars, and the entire temple fell crashing in on everyone inside, including the lords of the Philistines. Samson may have died with the Philistines, but he went to a different place than they did. The Bible tells you that Samson killed more Philistines in his death than he killed during his whole life.

The family of Samson came for his body, and buried him between Zorah and Eshtaol, the same place where the Spirit first moved upon him. The Bible says, *"Having begun in the Spirit, are you now being made perfect by the flesh?"* (Galatians 3:3). Samson drifted away from the Spirit in the prime of his life, but he still ended in the Spirit, and you can, too. He began in the Spirit, got in the flesh, but ended in the Spirit.

Let's remember that after our identities have been dedicated to God, He wants to stay the master over our weaknesses. Make God your *Adonai*, the divine director and master of your life's beginning, middle, and end.

Chapter Eight

Identity Change Brings Appetite for the Word

:::

It's exciting to know the impact that God's Word has on an identity that has been resurrected in Christ. It is so much greater than the impact on an identity that is up-and-down, in-and-out, and does not know its authority over Satan.

Nehemiah chapter eight is about the revival that God's Word brought to the people after they had dedicated themselves to God. This chapter is one of the few in the Bible where the people could eat fat and drink sweet drinks (see verse 10). It's a chapter that is full of calories! Throughout the Bible, especially in Proverbs, you find many warnings about foods, such as, "Don't be a glutton," or "Don't eat too many sweets." But I think it's interesting that in the chapter about God's Word, the people feasted on the fat and the sweet.

In this chapter, the walls of Jerusalem had been rebuilt, and her gates had been restored. Now the people were concerned, not with building anymore, but with hearing God's Word. In our lives, once the building has been done, God says, "Here is an identity that was restored by the Holy Spirit. Now it is ready to receive my Word in fullness through the Water Gate."

> *Now all the people gathered together as one man in the open square that was in front of the Water Gate; and they told Ezra the scribe to bring the Book of the Law of Moses, which the* LORD *had commanded Israel.*
>
> (NEHEMIAH 8:1)

Notice that the people read God's Word by the Water Gate, because in your identity, that is the gate through which you receive the Word. Once God's people began receiving the Word through this gate, they experienced revival. Why? Because if you love

Identity Change Brings Appetite for the Word

God's Word and have an expectancy towards it, you have reviving power!

The Word Brings Revival

The Israelites had a tremendous, positive attitude toward God's Word. First of all, you see that they reverenced it: *"And Ezra opened the book in the sight of all the people, for he was standing above all the people; and when he opened it, all the people stood up"* (Nehemiah 8:5).

People whose identities have been repaired by the Holy Spirit experience a new reverence and appreciation for God's Word. Nehemiah tells you that Ezra and the priests, however, did more than just read the Word — they explained what it meant to the people:

> *... And the Levites, helped the people to understand the Law; and the people stood in their place. So they read distinctly from the book, in the Law of God; and they gave the sense, and helped them to understand the reading.*
>
> (NEHEMIAH 8:7-8)

Basically, teaching God's Word is simply the practice of making it understandable to those hearing it, so that they can apply it to their lives. Ezra said, "It's great that you are listening to the Word, but you also have to receive and understand it so that you can practice it in your lives." The Word is not just to be read. It is to be applied to everything we do!

I have found that an identity with a positive attitude toward God's Word is the one that receives the most from it:

> *Nehemiah, who was the governor, Ezra the priest and scribe, and the Levites who taught the people said to all the people, "This day is holy to the* Lord *your God; do not mourn nor weep." For all the people wept, when they heard the words of the Law.* (NEHEMIAH 8:9)

The children of Israel were so deeply touched by the Word of God that it moved them to tears. These people reverenced God's Word, so they began to understand it. Then the Word of God moved their hearts, first to tears, and then to great joy:

Identity Change Brings Appetite for the Word

> *Then he said to them, "Go your way, eat the fat, drink the sweet, and send portions to those for whom nothing is prepared; for this day is holy to our Lord. Do not sorrow, for the joy of the L*ORD *is your strength."*
> (NEHEMIAH 8:10)

Hearing the Word brings joy to your heart! I love the words of Ezra: "Don't weep. Today is your day to be happy in the Word!" You know, many times in counseling I have come across people who have used the Word for condemnation rather than conviction and help. But God did not send His Word to condemn us. He sent it to convict and convince us that He truly loves us.

Nehemiah said, "Don't mourn. Don't be put down by the Word. Let it lift you up and fill your hearts with joy."

We have often sung, "The joy of the Lord is my strength." We just love that little chorus. But have we realized where the joy of the Lord and our strength are found? They are found in His Word. God's Word was meant to be our direct source of joy. Any man, woman, or child who gets involved in the Word will be involved in joy. Any person who reverences the Word is going to start rejoicing. Any person who respects and worships the Word will find that the joy of the Lord is his strength.

But Nehemiah did not just say, "Go and be joyful." He said, "Send portions to others." In other words, "Share what you have." We, as Christians, are supposed to enjoy the sweetness of God's Word. But God says, "Don't just be a hog about the Word and not do anything else. Share it with people who don't have it."

When you share the Word of God with other people, you receive even more joy. You cannot share Jesus without experiencing increased joy. I have observed that in my personal life, I love my quiet study time in God's Word. But then God wants to complete my joy by causing me to share His Word with others. He also wants to allow me to see His Word work in other people's lives. As I write this, I am believing for avenues to share the Word in different countries, such as Bangladesh, future work in Saudi Arabia, and Iran. God is opening doors that no man can shut!

Identity Change Brings Appetite for the Word

You say, "I'm joyful because I had a wonderful answer to prayer." Yes, but that is only temporary joy. God's Word brings permanent joy. Once, in Billings, Montana, a Methodist woman at one of my meetings received Christ as her savior. Afterward, she came to me and said, "My husband is in the hospital. Do you ever make hospital calls to pray for people?"

I told her, "I would be happy to pray for him."

I found out that the woman's husband had been a senator. One day, during a senate meeting, he fell backward to the floor, was taken to a hospital, and there his surgeons discovered that he had a brain tumor. The woman said, "He is in a coma and the doctors doubt that his condition will ever improve."

Revival never fails to flow when you share God's Word with other people.

The devil said to me, "If you pray for him, he will die. You need Oral Roberts or Kathryn Kuhlman for this. You need someone who is really powerful in God. Who are you?"

I fixed my thoughts on Mark 16:18, "[Believers] *will lay hands on the sick, and they will recover.*" I thought,

God's Word says that when believers lay hands on sick people, they will recover. It's my part to lay hands on people. God will take care of the rest.
When I arrived at the man's hospital room, his appearance was really sad. His eye was bandaged and there were tubes in his nose. I laid my hands on the man and commanded the spirits of death to leave. Then I prayed that the man's healing would bring glory to the name of Jesus.

But when God's Word is constantly flowing through your life, its refreshing overwhelms enemy fire.

When I prayed for the woman's husband to be healed, the devil said, "You didn't have faith when you prayed." But I just clung to Mark 16:18. I said, "God says that when I lay hands on sick people, they will recover." I left the hospital room and returned home the following day.

Just one month later, the woman who had asked me to pray for her husband called me to say, "My husband's health has done a complete turnaround since you prayed." He was no longer comatose. The man

Identity Change Brings Appetite for the Word

was eating, drinking, and walking; all of his bodily functions were near normal.

Jesus is so good! He wants to do more than just save our bodies — He also wants to save our souls. That autumn, my husband and I traveled back to Billings, Montana, and Wally visited the man for whom I had prayed. He was still in the hospital, so Wally sat with him and read Scriptures aloud. On that day, the man accepted Christ, right there in the hospital bed! The last I heard, the man traveled, worked, and was growing spiritually.

What brought life into that man's heart and physical body? The Word, the Word, the Word! Revival never fails to flow when you share God's Word with other people.

If you need a revival of joy inside, feast on the Word of God!

You may say, "I have revival, and my identity has already been repaired." But you need a continuous input of God's Word inside. Sometimes the devil comes to knock holes in the walls of your identity. He tries to throw fiery darts at your gates of authority to set them on fire. But when God's Word is constantly flowing through your life, its refreshing overwhelms enemy fire. Only through continuing in God's Word will you advance from one victory to the next. Only then can you enjoy the abundance of benefits intended for you in the Word.

As I ended my study on the Israelites' revival near the Water Gate, the Lord said, "The revival took place in the seventh month, and seven is the number of completion. My Word brought the people completion in their identities."

If you need a revival of joy inside, feast on the Word of God! In it you will find a river of consistent joy that can complete any area of your life: *"All the days of the afflicted are evil, but he who is of a merry heart has a continual feast"* (Proverbs 15:15).

Chapter Nine

Resurrection Bread to Feed Your Identity

:::

Sometimes we look at ourselves and say, "I'll never change. My mother and father were failures, and I'll be a failure." Then we pull out a long, long list of what we are and what we are not. But if you are a Christian who is feeding on the Word of God, you can receive resurrection power to make your identity rise above failure just as Jesus rose from death and ascended into the heavenlies.

Resurrection Power

Resurrection power is one of the most exciting things that God has for your identity. You received it when you were born again, and it was given to you for the purpose of transforming your soul. No wonder Philippians 2:13 can say, *"It is God who works in you both to will and to do for His good pleasure."* His work of resurrection within you delights Him and benefits you.

I never gave much thought to resurrection power until a woman shared with me her revelation on what the Bible says about leavened and unleavened bread. Her words so provoked me that I couldn't wait to get home to look up the references!

You may wonder, *What in the world does bread have to do with my identity?* It has a lot to do with your identity! You are going to be thrilled at how God has put resurrection power at work in your spirit for your soul — your identity — and your body. You can see a picture of that work in both the Old and New Testaments.

On the night the Israelites departed from Egypt, they ate unleavened bread with a lamb that had been roasted by fire. Before that first Passover meal, all leaven had been removed from every Hebrew house. In this case, and in many cases in the Bible, the unleavened bread was representative of sinlessness. The people were to clean out the sin from their lives before God could move on their behalf.

Not only did God have the people eat unleavened bread at the time of their exodus from Egypt, but they also ate unleavened bread when God gave His commands about sacrifices. Any blood from sacrifices was to be offered with unleavened bread because God did not want sin involved whatsoever.

In the New Testament, Jesus said, *"I am the bread of life"* (John 6:35). We all know that Jesus said those words about Himself, but how often do we relate His words to the miracle in which He multiplied five loaves and two fish to feed 5,000 people? First, Jesus multiplied the food. Then, He fed the multitudes.

> *"Most assuredly, I say to you, Moses did not give you the bread from heaven, but My Father gives you the true bread from heaven.*

For the bread of God is He who comes down from heaven and gives life to the world."
(JOHN 6:32-33)

I was sure that in this passage of Scripture, Jesus must have been talking about unleavened bread. But to my shock, when I studied the Greek, He was speaking of leavened bread! That bread has yeast in it. Does leavened bread come from heaven? I thought that perhaps in my study, there had been an error, so I quickly referred back to the Old Testament to look up some more Scriptures.

I thought, *Lord, where did they eat leavened bread as opposed to unleavened bread?* I found out that in the Old Testament, there were two times when leavened bread was to be eaten by the people of Israel. Amos 4:5 says:

> *"Offer a sacrifice of thanksgiving with leaven,*
> *Proclaim and announce the freewill offerings;*
> *For this you love,*
> *You children of Israel!"*
> *Says the* LORD *God.*

When the sons of Israel made a thanksgiving offering, in which they thanked God for all His works in their lives, their offering contained leaven. I thought, *How interesting that offerings of thanks have rising power!* Looking further, I found that on the day of Pentecost, also known as the Feast of Harvest or of Weeks (Exodus 23:16; 34:22), two huge loaves of bread were baked for the feast day (Leviticus 23:17), and those loaves contained leaven. God said, "When you give thanksgiving, and when you celebrate Pentecost, use leavened bread."

The right kind of leaven will increase the work of God in your life. But the wrong kind of leaven will increase the devil's work.

Why use leaven if it is a type of sin? The study was beginning to confuse me instead of making sense, so I studied further in the New Testament to see what God had to say about leavened bread. One Scripture was a parable in Matthew: *"The kingdom of heaven is like leaven, which a woman took and hid in three measures of meal till it was all leavened"* (Matthew 13:33).

We can't say there is anything wrong with the kingdom of heaven, can we? God wouldn't compare the kingdom of heaven with a type of sin. I found out that there is more than one type of leaven. In Luke 12:1, Jesus said, *"Beware of the leaven of the Pharisees"* and indicated again that leaven is a type of sin — in this case, that of wrong doctrine. But there is a right kind of leaven that has rising power to cause a Christian's life to flourish and be fruitful. The right kind of leaven will increase the work of God in your life. But the wrong kind of leaven will increase the devil's work.

When the devil places leaven in a man's heart, whether it is false doctrine or some other kind of sin, that sin begins to spread. Sin doesn't stop with "one little, tiny sin." It multiplies into more. That is why it is so important that we dedicate ourselves to works of righteousness every day.

In 1 Corinthians 5:7, Paul exhorted his brethren, *"Therefore purge out the old leaven, that you may be a new lump."* He was speaking of immorality in the church — the devil's leaven.

Paul, however, knew the power of heavenly leaven. In Acts 27, he was sailing on a ship with unbelievers

Resurrection Bread to Feed Your Identity

when a terrible storm threatened to overwhelm them all. They lightened the load as much as possible. They were so wearied, they didn't even eat! Later an angel appeared to Paul and reassured him that they would not perish but would run aground. After two weeks, he encouraged them to eat. He then took some leavened bread, thanked God, and ate it. The men then ate some food as well. It is interesting that Paul did not eat meat. Instead, he ate leavened bread.

I believe that Paul, in eating leavened bread, was making a statement: "I am taking the bread of Jesus Christ that brings me resurrection power." If you're wondering how I can make that conclusion, I found it in John 6:32–33. Jesus spoke of Himself:

> *Then Jesus said to them, "Most assuredly, I say to you, Moses did not give you the bread from heaven, but My Father gives you the true bread from heaven. For the bread of God is He who comes down from heaven and gives life to the world."*

Jesus Christ is our leavened bread to give us divine life!

I wondered, *What kind of bread did Jesus give His disciples in the Last Supper?* The Scripture says, "*[Jesus] took bread, gave thanks and broke it, and gave it to them, saying, 'This is My body which is given for you; do this in remembrance of Me'*" (Luke 22:19). At the Last Supper, Jesus gave His disciples leavened bread. It represented His body, which would rise from the grave in only a few days to give life to the world. He was saying, "I am going to die, but I am going to rise as well, and through my death you will eat of my resurrection."

The disciples were partaking of leavened bread because they were esteeming the resurrection of Christ.

John 6:50 says, "*This is the bread which comes down from heaven, that one may eat of it and not die.*" When you eat of Jesus, the Bread of Life, you eat of resurrection power and will never taste eternal death.

In Mark 7:26–27, a woman whose daughter had an unclean spirit came and fell at Jesus's feet to ask for His mercy on her daughter:

Resurrection Bread to Feed Your Identity

The woman was a Greek, a Syro-Phoenician by birth, and she kept asking Him to cast the demon out of her daughter. But Jesus said to her, "Let the children be filled first, for it is not good to take the children's bread and throw it to the little dogs."

What kind of bread was Jesus speaking of in this text? He was talking about leavened bread. What is the "children's bread?" It is resurrection power! The children of God must have the Bread of Life if their lives are to bring forth the resurrection power of God to help others. That life in them causes healing and transformation for others.

The disciples learned the power of resurrection through leavened bread as they tarried together before Pentecost: *"And they continued steadfastly in the apostles' doctrine and fellowship, in the breaking of bread, and in prayers"* (Acts 2:42). The disciples were partaking of leavened bread because they were esteeming the resurrection of Christ. The more they ate of Jesus, the more resurrection power filled the room!

There was a feast of unleavened bread in the New Testament (Passover), but there was also a very strong revelation of the importance of leavened bread. It is so important that we esteem the leaven of the kingdom and let it grow and multiply in our hearts. As resurrection power grows in our hearts, it reaches forth and extends that power to those around us.

In 1 Corinthians 10:16-17, Paul unfolded a very deep revelation about partaking of resurrection bread when we take Communion:

> *The cup of blessing which we bless, is it not the communion of the blood of Christ? The bread which we break, is it not the communion of the body of Christ? For we, though many, are one bread and one body; for we all partake of that one bread.*

When you take Communion, you partake of the benefit of bringing supernatural life into your mind, your body, and your spirit — your identity. Jesus wanted that power to fill your whole being!

Gone Fishin'

John 21 records that Jesus appeared to His disciples after His resurrection and caused them to catch so many fish that they could not pull the net from the water. On the shore of the Sea of Galilee, where Jesus cooked the fish over a fire, He also gave His disciples bread. Peter had returned to the fishing trade and had taken most of the disciples with him. All of them had left behind the work of the gospel to become fishermen again. That seems like a terrible thing to do, but Jesus knew how to bring them back: He gave them the bread of resurrection power!

Peter had been struggling on the fishing boat all night and had not caught a single fish. We really know how to struggle, don't we? Then a man stood on the shore. "Children," the man called, "Have you anything to eat?"

The disciples shouted back, "No, we worked all night and didn't catch a thing."

Jesus called back, "Cast your nets to the other side." The disciples still didn't recognize Him, but they did as He had said. You see, sometimes a person standing ashore can spot the darkened areas of the water where entire schools of fish are swimming. When the disciples cast their nets on the other side, there were so many fish that they hardly knew what to do! At that moment, John recognized that the man on the shore was Jesus, and Peter jumped into the sea and swam to Jesus.

When Peter saw Jesus, he grabbed the whole load of fish and hauled it to the shore by himself! Somehow, in the presence of Jesus, Peter could do what six men could not. Peter was tasting of resurrection power. Peter had been very defeated, and at that point in his life, all he could see was failure. He had denied Jesus, so then he wondered, *What's the use of going on? I'm no disciple.* Have you ever felt that way? Have you blown it royally and now you wonder, *Why bother?* Jesus wants to lift you out of that depression and bring you into resurrection power and renew your identity.

When Peter came to the shore, Jesus didn't say, "Peter, I want to talk about how you denied me. Not only did you deny me, but you returned to the fishing trade and left the ministry to which I called you." Jesus didn't rebuke Peter. Instead, Jesus led Peter into resurrection power to transform his life.

Resurrection Bread to Feed Your Identity

Jesus said, "Peter, I fixed you a meal." Peter was cold from his impromptu swim from the boat and tired from trying unsuccessfully all night to catch fish. He was undoubtedly hungry. He also felt defeated. Jesus fed Peter and the rest of the disciples with some of the fish they had caught. The Lord was concerned about their physical needs as well as their spiritual needs. By feeding the disciples leavened bread, with the fish, Jesus was saying, "I am preparing you to participate in resurrection."

Then Jesus began to ask Peter some questions. Jesus asked, "Peter, do you love me?" Jesus was asking, "Peter, do you *agape* me?" *Agape* is the kind of love with which God loves us.

Peter answered, "Lord, you know I love you," and there the word love is "*phileō*," meaning the reciprocal love and affection between friends. Peter was saying, "You love me, and I also love you."

Jesus told Peter, "Feed my sheep." Then He asked, "Peter, do you love (*agape*) me?"

Again, Peter said, "Lord, you know I love (*phileō*) you."

Jesus said, "Feed my lambs."

Then for a third time, Jesus asked Peter, "Do you love me?" This time, the word "love" that Jesus used was *phileō*, meaning "reciprocal love." Why did Jesus ask Peter three times? I think there are a number of factors involved here that show how Jesus led Peter back into resurrection power.

You see, Peter had denied the Lord three times, so Jesus asked three times, "Do you love me?" When Peter denied Jesus, Peter was warming his hands over the enemy's fire. Now, as he stood with Jesus by another fire, the memories certainly must have rushed back to Peter's mind. But Jesus hadn't come to put Peter down. Jesus wanted to bring leavened bread to make Peter rise above past defeats.

When Jesus used the word *phileō* (reciprocal love), He was saying, "Peter, you can feed my sheep even if you only love me reciprocally."

Why, then, did Jesus first emphasize *agape* love? Because those who are involved in feeding God's Word to the body of Christ must expect nothing back. You may feed sheep who will turn against you, hate you, despise you, and lie about you, as Judas did to the Lord. Despite those things, you still have to

Resurrection Bread to Feed Your Identity

love in return. Only God's love, *agape* love, is capable of loving in that way.

Jesus was saying, "Peter, I am giving you resurrection bread because you will return to the ministry, and you will need rising power. You must love me with a love that expects nothing back." Then Jesus prophesied about the love that Peter would need to have:

> *"Most assuredly, I say to you, when you were younger, you girded yourself and walked where you wished; but when you are old, you will stretch out your hands, and another will gird you and carry you where you do not wish."* (JOHN 21:18)

Jesus was saying, "Peter, because of my resurrection power in you, you are going to love me and the church so greatly that you will be willing to die for us. Peter, somebody is going to take you where you don't want to go, and they will stretch out your hands." Historians say that Peter was crucified for his faith, and when the men crucified him, he said, "Don't crucify me like Jesus. I am not worthy to die like Him," so Peter was crucified upside-down. He had fed the Lord's sheep with *agape* love that expected nothing in return.

Jesus ended His prophecy to Peter with the words, "Follow me." How could Peter follow the Lord unto death, having denied him before? Peter had resurrection bread, so he had partaken of life and power.

Jesus placed His own life, resurrection power, in you when you were saved. Every time you take Communion, remember that you are taking Jesus's life and ability to rise over any hindrances to your identity. You are taking resurrection power, the leavened bread of Christ.

Jesus doesn't want your identity to be defeated. Peter was defeated, but he overcame it to the point that he was even martyred for the Lord. He died victoriously and was welcomed into heavenly places with the Lord. That same victory in which Peter overcame is the victory that is in your heart and life through Jesus Christ. Let your identity rise into the Lord's high calling for you.

Chapter Ten

Your Identity Can Draw Interest

:::

In studying Nehemiah, you have seen the importance of the gates of authority in your identity. You saw the repair of the walls and the hanging of the gates, and you saw that, even though completed, the city was still subject to attack. God says, "Just because the walls are up, it does not mean that you will never have another attack against your identity."

Then you looked at how dedication of your identity to God is important, including daily dedication to Him. We need to dedicate our actions and reactions so that we will handle every situation the way He wants us to handle it.

By now, you have seen the necessary parts of bringing your identity together and keeping it yielded to God. But never forget that, throughout your life, God will continually deal with you about your identity. It is important to heed what He says.

Sometimes we think, *God isn't even bothering to deal with me.* But He is. I saw this in the lives of Abraham and Sarah.

Abraham and Sarah

Thinking about Sarah always makes me chuckle because the Bible is very plain about the qualities of her humanity. Sarah wanted a baby so badly! In her day, it was considered a disgrace not to have a baby, so I'm sure that pride was a part of the problem. But she also had a woman's natural desire for children. However, Sarah was physically unable to have children.

God promised Sarah and Abraham a child, but for years that child didn't come. Being human and not having her identity totally submitted to God, Sarah hatched up something that she imagined to be a terrific plan. She said, "Abraham, I have a great idea. Since I haven't had children, maybe God would use my handmaiden to give you a child. Then she could turn the child over to me, and it would be ours. This could be the child that God promised."

Abraham listened to this beautiful wife of his. The Bible tells you that she was really a knockout, she was so stunning. Sarah convinced him of her plan, and not long afterward, Hagar, Sarah's handmaiden, had Abraham's child.

After the child was born, Sarah was no longer excited about the idea. Instead, you find old, human Sarah. She was jealous. Of course, she was jealous! Wouldn't you be jealous if your husband had a child by some other woman, and they brought it to you to be raised? Not to mention that the child would be a reminder of your husband's relationship with someone else!

Day in and day out, Hagar and Sarah shared the same kitchen. It doesn't work today, it didn't work then, and it wasn't in God's plan. Sarah complained to Abraham, who basically gave Sarah free reign, saying, *"Do to her as you please"* (Genesis 16:6). Sarah really became harsh then with Hagar, and Hagar said, "I don't have to take this." And she ran away.

After an angelic visitation in which the angel told Hagar she would have a son and to name the baby Ishmael, a much more submissive Hagar was accepted back into Sarah's household.

Finally, the time arrived for Abraham and Sarah to have a child. Three divine visitors came to announce God's plan to Abraham, and he knew they were from God. Meanwhile, Sarah was inside the tent eavesdropping. One of the visitors said to Abraham, "You are going to have a son," and inside the tent, Sarah laughed to herself. She thought that it was hilarious because she and Abraham were both past the age of childbearing. They probably had no physical relationship anymore, so how could there be a baby? Then the divine visitor asked Abraham, "Why did your wife laugh?" Sarah opened the tent door and said, "Oh, I didn't laugh." Just like a woman. But she did have the baby.

Hebrews 11 really compliments Sarah by saying that she had faith for the strength she needed to have a baby. Don't say that Abraham had all the faith just because Sarah laughed. Sarah had faith for the strength she needed. I looked up the Greek word for strength, and it is *dunamis*, or "miracle-working power." Sarah, in all her human frailty, also had faith. She had faith that God would give her a child, and He gave her a baby whose name was Isaac. I think that God really has a sense of humor because the child's name means "laughter." Maybe God said, "I had the last laugh, didn't I, Sarah? You laughed in unbelief, but I laugh because my promises really are true and real."

How good God is! How exciting and patient, because He takes us right where we are — just the raw material — and begins molding our identities in spite of our failures. Aren't you glad that He never gives up?

Eli and His Sons

Although God does not give up, we can choose to live our lives in a constant battle by not allowing the Holy Spirit to lead and guide us. The enemy is always around, trying to lead us in a different direction than that of God's. I looked at the life of a man named Eli and saw a tragedy that did not have to happen.

Eli was a godly man, but he did not stand against the devil's attacks. Though he recognized and was warned about those attacks, his reprimands of his sons were to no avail.

The name "Eli" means "lofty" and he was an outstanding priest who loved God's work and did not shirk his priestly responsibilities. The people counseled with Eli, prayed with him, and he offered sacrifices for them. You say, "He sounds wonderful."

But you can be wonderful in your service to God and neglectful of the other areas of your life. We need to respond to whatever area God is dealing with, and in Eli's case, the problem was with his two sons, Hophni and Phinehas.

When you see the names of Eli's two sons, you begin to see how important our dealings with our children can be. I remember one time when I was having difficulty with my own young son, shortly after my husband and I adopted him. I prayed, "Lord, why have you given me a child when my attitude is so poor?" He said, "Marilyn, there are some things that I can only teach you through a child." That was a real shocker! Everyone who is a parent, however, will say "amen" to that 1,000 times!

Eli had two children whom God wanted to use in molding and shaping his identity. Hophni means "a

Your Identity Can Draw Interest

pair of fists," and Phinehas means "mouth of a serpent." I think the first was a rebel, and the second was a liar. I have seen both rebellion and dishonesty in my own children, and I can't stand either of them. But you can't ignore them. You have to deal with them. Eli, however, didn't deal with the problems that his sons presented.

In the beginning of the first book of Samuel, a woman came to the temple where Eli ministered as a priest, and there was a great contrast between her and Eli. The woman, Hannah, had no children but desperately wanted them. She had a husband who adored her and would have done anything for her, but she was not satisfied with just his love. She wanted a baby.

Hannah's husband had another wife who had given him children, but the Bible tells you that he loved Hannah more than the other wife. Seemingly, Hannah just couldn't get over her barrenness, which the other wife would not let her forget.

One day, at the time of the yearly sacrifice, Hannah's husband, Elkanah, brought his wives and children to Shiloh, and when they arrived, Hannah went to the tabernacle, which was in Shiloh. There she prayed silently, "God, give me a child." Her prayer was very specific:

> "O LORD of hosts, if You will indeed look on the affliction of Your maidservant and remember me, and not forget Your maidservant, but will give Your maidservant a male child, then I will give him to the LORD all the days of his life, and no razor shall come upon his head." (1 SAMUEL 1:11)

As Hannah prayed, she travailed so much that Eli walked over and said, *"How long will you be drunk? Put your wine away from you!"* (1 Samuel 1:14). Hannah wasn't drunk; she was just upset. My first reaction to Eli's statement would be to tell him, "It's none of your business saying anything to Hannah, because you don't correct your own children. You correct a woman for drinking, but you won't correct your sons for doing the same thing!"

But I want you to see the unfolding of God's plan in these two identities. One of the identities was willing to respond to situations in God's way. The other was not. Eli was a priest, yet he refused God's dealings with his children. Hannah received the dealing of God.

When Eli confronted Hannah, she answered, "I'm not drunk. I'm sorrowful in spirit." Then Eli spoke some words that were full of faith: "*Go in peace, and the God of Israel grant your petition which you have asked of Him*" (I Samuel 1:17).

When Eli spoke those words, Hannah believed them. She went to eat at the feast of the peace offering with the rest of her family. The next morning, they rose early to worship and then went home. Then the Lord remembered Hannah and she conceived her child; she had a beautiful little boy whom she named "Samuel," meaning "heard of God."

Hannah said, "I am going to keep this child until he is weaned, and then I will give him back to God. He will be loaned to God all his life."

I looked at Hannah and thought, *Imagine having just one child, one beautiful boy*, which I imagine Samuel was. I thought, *After Samuel was weaned, she gave that boy to Eli, who knew absolutely nothing about raising children.*

He let his boys rebel all their lives. When they became priests, they still rebelled by committing adultery with the women who sought spiritual counsel, by drinking strong drink, and eating the fat from the sacrifices.

How could Hannah send her gift from God into that environment? From looking at natural circumstances, we would say, "That's going to ruin Samuel's identity! He is so young and impressionable." But because Hannah had loaned Samuel to the Lord, Samuel was no longer her responsibility. He was God's responsibility, and God blessed him.

Everyone wants to get spiritual when they experience troubles. I am not against that, because trouble has brought many people to God.

Hannah left her son at the tabernacle with Eli, and she saw her child each year, when she brought him a new, little coat that she had made for him. She was true to her vow, and the story shows that anything you give to God draws interest, because God gave Hannah five more children!

As Samuel grew, God began dealing with Eli, and of all people, God dealt with him through the child.

Your Identity Can Draw Interest

One evening, when Samuel was just a little boy, he heard a voice as he slept, "Samuel, Samuel!" The child thought that Eli was calling, so he ran to the priest and asked, "Did you call me?" Eli said, "I didn't call you. Go back to bed."

Samuel went back to bed, and then the voice spoke his name again. Again, he asked the priest, "Did you call me?" Samuel received the same answer as before, so he went to sleep again. Again, he heard the voice.

Eli was definitely a spiritually perceptive man. He had perceived faith in Hannah and told her to receive her son. Now he perceived that the voice Samuel heard was the Lord speaking to him. Eli told the child that the next time he heard the voice, he should say, *"Speak, Lord, for Your servant hears"* (1 Samuel 3:9).

Samuel went back to his room, and when the voice spoke to him, "Samuel," he said, *"Speak, Lord, for Your servant hears."* Instead of receiving a positive, uplifting message from the Lord, the first thing Samuel heard was negative!

> *Then the Lord said to Samuel... "In that day I will perform against Eli all that I have spoken concerning his house, from beginning*

> to end. For I have told him that I will judge his house forever for the iniquity which he knows, because his sons made themselves vile, and he did not restrain them. And therefore I have sworn to the house of Eli that the iniquity of Eli's house shall not be atoned for by sacrifice or offering forever."
>
> (1 SAMUEL 3:11-14)

God was basically saying, "Eli honored his children above me." How terrible it is that Eli put his children first! God teaches us through our children, and God had warned Eli about his children before. Yet Eli ignored God's dealings and chose to let the boys go their own ways.

The morning after God spoke to Samuel, the boy woke up, not wanting to tell Eli what had been said. But Eli asked, "What did God tell you? Don't hold anything back from me. I will not be angry with you."

Samuel told him what God said: "You put your children above God, so God is going to cut you off, and cut off your children from the priesthood." This could have been a real turning point for Eli; he could have taken the opportunity to conform his identity to

God's plans. Yet, while this deeply saddened Samuel, Eli accepted God's judgment — and did nothing.

After this incident, Samuel really began to grow in the Lord and in ministry toward the people. Meanwhile, the Philistines came on the scene and began abusing the people of Israel, and the people were very backslidden. It appears that, just as Eli had never corrected his sons, neither had he corrected the people. Spiritually, things looked bad, and everyone wondered what to do.

Everyone wants to get spiritual when they experience troubles. I am not against that, because trouble has brought many people to God. But we should get spiritual *before* trouble comes, and then maybe it wouldn't be so troublesome!

One day, Israel went out to battle against the Philistines. The people said, "Let's get the ark of the covenant and take it into the battle." When the Philistines heard that the Israelites were bringing out the ark, they said, *"God has come into the camp! . . . Woe to us!"* (1 Samuel 4:7). The Philistines knew that they would have to really fight against Israel.

The Philistines raced out, fought hard, and won the battle against Israel. They captured the ark, and Eli's sons, Hophni and Phinehas, were killed. It wasn't long before the news circulated back to Eli.

By this time, Eli was a very fat old man. You may get mad at me for this, and if you do, I hope you'll forgive me; but I don't think that God ignores fat on our bodies. He is concerned when we don't discipline our physical bodies because it may indicate a lack of discipline in other areas of our lives.

Eli heard about the news of his sons' deaths and what happened to the ark of the covenant. The men reporting the news told Eli, "The ark was captured by the Philistines." Of course, Eli's prime concern was the ark of the covenant, which does give some credit to his spiritual desires. But if you won't let God move in all the areas of your identity, you can ruin the other areas. Upon hearing that the ark of the covenant had been taken, Eli fell over backward and broke his neck.

If you follow the line of Eli's priesthood further, you will find that God ended the entire priesthood from the lineage of Eli. He completely cut off that household because of the intentional overindulgence and disobedience that had taken place. Why? Because Eli would not allow God to have full dominion over a certain area of his identity. God doesn't want our service. He wants all of us. Service for God will be a fruit coming from our submission to God.

Samuel

What happened to Samuel? He became the priest. He was a beautiful example of a priest, for he traveled, ministered, and counseled the people. But then one day, the people came to Samuel and said, "All the other nations have kings, but we have you, a judge, prophet, and priest. We want a king, too."

Listening to this, Samuel was hurt. Samuel brought the hurt to God, and He said, "Don't take it personally. They haven't rejected you; they have rejected me. If they want a king, let them have a king."

Samuel anointed a king named Saul, who never allowed his identity to be subjected to God. Saul was really a rebel! The walls and gates of his identity were full of holes, and he never listened to God. Finally, God dealt with Saul and said that the kingdom would be taken from him.

Even though Saul was such a selfish man, Samuel still loved him and said, "God forbid that I should ever cease to pray for you."

We want to say, "Samuel, this man took your place! He pushed you out of being the leader." But Samuel knew that the people hadn't rejected him. They had rejected God. And God never takes you from one position without giving you another. He gave Samuel the greatest ministry of his life by calling him to start a prophet's school.

Samuel returned to his hometown, Ramah, and probably on the land he inherited from his parents, he stepped up in the plan of God. Today, when you read about all of the exciting prophets of the Old Testament (including Elijah, Elisha, and Nathan), I believe all of them came from a school that was started by Samuel.

Hannah probably looked down from heaven and smiled when she saw Samuel training future prophets. I know that Hannah was glad she "loaned" Samuel to the Lord because her loan is still drawing interest today. That's a high interest rate!

Let your identity be under God's complete control. God wants your identity to draw heavenly interest rates too, and it will when it is totally submitted to Him.

Chapter Eleven

Two Confessions for a Balanced Identity

:::

Your words probably have more to do with the condition of your identity than any other one thing. The Bible tells you so, very plainly, in Proverbs 18:21: *"Death and life are in the power of the tongue, and those who love it will eat its fruit."*

In other words, people who understand the importance of their words are going to be speaking fruitful words with their tongues. Your words, your confessions of faith, and the confessing of sin to find freedom, should be the "last word" in maintaining an identity that is balanced by God's Word.

Confession of Sin

When I look at the word "confession," the first thing I think of is the confession of sins. First John 1:9 tells us, *"If we confess our sins, He is faithful and just to forgive us our sins and to cleanse us from all unrighteousness."* I think it is so great that God not only forgives us but He also cleanses us! He even wants to clean out the desires that caused us to enter areas of sin.

Forgiveness can only come after confession, and through that process we are cleansed.

I have often seen that sin may result from hurts in the past. For example, a girl who is sexually abused in her youth may become a prostitute. Sin may also result from divorce; a man may take revenge on his ex-wife, maybe even kill her. Sin may even be the result of a generational curse — someone says, "My grandfather and father were alcoholics, and now I'm one." But God is such a good, forgiving God. In His own words, He told us:

Two Confessions for a Balanced Identity

"... For I, the LORD your God, am a jealous God, visiting the iniquity of the fathers upon the children to the third and fourth generations of those who hate Me, but showing mercy to thousands, to those who love Me and keep My commandments."

(EXODUS 20:5-6)

A lot of the junk in our lives starts in our homes; that's the "iniquity," and it continues for three or four generations of those who hate God. But you don't hate Him, or you wouldn't be reading this now. You love Him and if you love Him, He will bless your descendants to a thousand generations! So blessing is much greater than the curse. The curse can only go to four generations at its best, but the blessing is so great for those who love Him, it can go to a thousand generations! I can think of certain things from my past that are now so far from my identity that I wonder, *How could I ever have done that?* But God showed me mercy and He cleansed me from those things.

In a previous chapter, we looked at David's involvement in the sins of adultery and murder. At first, he tried to cover up his sins and hide them. But even if you try to cover them up or hide them, God can bring them to light. David was a fallen man. But when Nathan, the prophet, exposed his sin, he didn't blame Bathsheba. He didn't make excuses. David didn't deny it. He confessed it. In fact, in Psalm 51, he wrote: *"For I acknowledge my transgressions, and my sin is always before me"* (v. 3). He was no longer a fallen man but a forgiven man, one whose descendant was Jesus Christ, the Son of God!

A weakness may even be a sin if it is something that bugs you and from which you want to be free. For example, people who smoke or are addicted to drugs are controlled by these weaknesses. What is your weakness? How can you get free from it? Begin by looking for the truth: *"Behold, You desire truth in the inward parts, and in the hidden part You will make me to know wisdom"* (Psalm 51:6). The Hebrew for "hidden part" is *ṭuḥâ* and refers to the "seat of wisdom" that is "in the heart."

You first have to identify the thing, the weakness, repent, and seek God's wisdom that will lead you to desire the truth regarding its resolution. Remember, repentance is a total 180-degree turning away from sin and a change of behavior. God is looking for change

Two Confessions for a Balanced Identity

not just in the physical realm but also in the inward parts of your heart. The best way to change is through storing up God's wisdom found in His Word in your heart. Trying to change yourself is very hard. You have to let go and let God. Follow David's example; he asked God to: *"Create in me a clean heart, O God, and renew a steadfast spirit within me"* (Psalm 51:10). Change is hard. Ask God to do it! Choose God's transformation. His process can make you stable, and one day at a time, you will be victorious for only He can turn your weaknesses into strengths.

When your heart gets free, you get free! Forgiveness can only come after confession, and through that process we are cleansed. Cleansing can lead to further development of your identity. David's identity was tied up in God's and he desired to do the will of God: "[God] *raised up for them David as king, to whom also He gave testimony and said, 'I have found David the son of Jesse, a man after My own heart, who will do all My will'* " (Acts 13:22). David was the best king and military commander Israel ever had.

What's cooking for you? Could it be something that *"Eye has not seen, nor ear heard, nor have entered into the heart of man the things which God has prepared for those who love Him"* (1 Corinthians 2:9)? Wouldn't you like to have God call you a man or woman after His own heart? That's an identity I would cherish, so I purpose to do His will!

Confession of Faith

The Bible also tells you that, along with the confession of sins, you can confess words to bring life. On one hand, you see that sin must be confessed in order for you to have a prosperous identity. Proverbs 28:13 tells you that a person who does not confess sin cannot prosper. But on the other hand, if all you did was walk around confessing sin, you would really be a negative person. God said, *"Death and life are in the power of the tongue"* (Proverbs 18:21). If you only confessed death, would you have life? No! You have to have both, so your second important confession is the confession of faith.

What is the confession of faith? It is the confession of God's Word for your life. There is great power in confessing God's Word after you confess sins, and you can see this in the ninth chapter of Nehemiah:

Two Confessions for a Balanced Identity

> *Now on the twenty-fourth day of this month the children of Israel were assembled with fasting, in sackcloth, and with dust on their heads. Then those of Israelite lineage separated themselves from all foreigners; and they stood and confessed their sins and the iniquities of their fathers.* (NEHEMIAH 9:1-2)

Notice that the people confessed their fathers' sins in addition to their own sins! Then they followed those confessions with reading the Word of God and confessing His goodness:

> *And they stood up in their place and read from the Book of the Law of the LORD their God for one-fourth of the day; and for another fourth they confessed and worshiped the LORD their God.* (NEHEMIAH 9:3)

I understand that the "part of the day" spoken of here means a 12-hour period (daytime hours), so it means that for three hours the people read God's Word. Then for the next three hours, they confessed the Lord and worshiped Him. Notice that they did these things after having confessed their sins. Both confessions must go together to help you maintain a balanced identity. The important thing is that your confession starts with God's Word.

> **The confession of sin and the confession of God's goodness in our lives are so powerful!**

God's Word acts as a mirror for both types of confession. The Word first brings repentance because it reveals any areas of sin in your life. After you see the sin, you repent and are cleansed from it. Then God's Word can show you who you are in Christ to build a positive foundation in that area of your identity. That is when your confession of faith comes in and you say, "I always triumph in Christ," or "I am more than a conqueror in Him." Speaking God's Word over your identity reinforces the walls so that they can stand against the enemy, should he attack again.

At the end of Nehemiah chapter nine, the Israelites made a covenant with God concerning their lives and identities. They committed themselves, their actions, and their words to God:

Two Confessions for a Balanced Identity

"Here we are, servants today!
And the land that You gave to our fathers,
To eat its fruit and its bounty,
Here we are, servants in it!
And it yields much increase to the kings
You have set over us,
Because of our sins;
Also they have dominion over
   our bodies and our cattle
At their pleasure;
And we are in great distress.

And because of all this,
We make a sure covenant and write it;
Our leaders, our Levites, and our
   priests seal it." (NEHEMIAH 9:36-38)

They said, "God, we are confessing our sins. We are also confessing that you are our God who will bring us through, so we make a covenant to keep our confessions right."

The confession of sin and the confession of God's goodness in our lives are so powerful! We need both to enhance our relationships with God. The book of Proverbs reveals even more about how your confession affects not only your identity but also your health: *"Pleasant words are like a honeycomb, sweetness to the soul and health to the bones"* (Proverbs 16:24). When you begin to say good things, you bring health to your soul — which is your mind, your emotions, and your will. Do you want a healthy mind and emotional reactions? Do you want a will that constantly chooses God's Word? Then confess the Word of God. It also brings physical health. Do you want a healthy body? Start saying pleasant things, because those words bring life into your physical body.

There is another side to this: *"Anxiety in the heart of man causes depression, but a good word makes it glad"* (Proverbs 12:25). If you're walking around saying ugly things about people and circumstances, then the person you are hurting the most is yourself. You are going to make your heart stop, and you are going to make other people's hearts stop. But you can switch your confession over to the positive and change the situation that was bothering you!

Two Confessions for a Balanced Identity

Elijah

In looking at the life of Elijah, I saw that his confessions consistently took him from one peak of faith to another. His name means "Yahweh is my God," and he was mightily used to show salvation to the nation of Israel during a terrible time of backsliding and sin.

In the book of Deuteronomy, God had set forth the conditions of blessings and curses to the children of Israel. God said, "If you obey my commandments, I will bless you; but if you break my laws, I will close the heavens and make them like bronze, and the earth like iron" (see Deuteronomy 28:23).

During the days of Elijah, Israel found out what God meant by those Scriptures! Elijah came on the scene as God's prophet after the people of Israel were falling into idolatry, led by their queen, a very wicked woman named Jezebel. Her husband's name was Ahab, and he did anything she wanted. He had a spine like a marshmallow! The people fell into idolatry and began to worship Baal, so God told Elijah, "I am closing the heavens, and it will not rain for three-and-a-half years."

> *Elijah the Tishbite, of the inhabitants of Gilead, said to Ahab, "As the LORD God of Israel lives, before whom I stand, there shall not be dew nor rain these years, except at my word."* (1 KINGS 17:1)

Ahab was not only a weak ruler; he also angered God: "*Ahab made a wooden image. Ahab did more to provoke the LORD God of Israel to anger than all the kings of Israel who were before him*" (1 Kings 16:33). But Elijah said, "The Lord God of Israel lives" and then prophesied a drought. Then he walked off, leaving Ahab standing there with his mouth hanging open.

After that prophecy, God led Elijah to a brook called Cherith, where he would be sustained for a time during the drought. While Elijah stayed at Cherith, the Lord ministered to him, and he drank from the brook. God also used ravens to bring Elijah his food. That seems interesting because, to the Jews, ravens were unclean birds. On top of that, you see that the ravens never ate Elijah's food, even though this was a time of drought. This was God's miracle and plan for Elijah.

Two Confessions for a Balanced Identity

After Elijah had stayed at Cherith for many days, the brook began to dry up. God had led Elijah to the brook, so what was wrong? Why would it dry up? When something like this happens, don't just race out and do some big thing on your own. Just hold on, and God will tell you what comes next. Elijah waited, and the Lord spoke to him again: *"Arise, go to Zarephath, which belongs to Sidon, and dwell there. See, I have commanded a widow there to provide for you"* (1 Kings 17:9).

I believe Zarephath probably wasn't Elijah's favorite place to go because it was part of Sidon, Jezebel's hometown (1 Kings 16:31). She wasn't living there at the time, but if she decided to visit her mother, aunt, or cousin, she might have run into Elijah. But Elijah didn't seem outwardly nervous. He just obeyed God's voice.

I imagine that Elijah thought the widow who would sustain him was probably loaded with money. He must have been shocked when, after arriving in Zarephath, he encountered a very poor widow who said, "I have only a bit of oil and flour, so I am making a cake for me and my son, and then we will die" (see 1 Kings 17:12).

That isn't exactly the kind of widow you would want taking care of you, is it? But she was God's provision for Elijah, and he knew it. He never looked to the widow for help, but instead he just looked to God and helped the widow look to Him also. Elijah said to her, "*Do not fear; go and do as you have said, but make me a small cake from it first, and bring it to me; and afterward make some for yourself and your son*" (1 Kings 17:13).

The woman barely had enough food for her son and herself! And Elijah wanted some, too? And he wanted the firstfruits as well? But she had to live by faith, so she baked the man of God his cake and brought it to him because Elijah had said, "*The bin of flour shall not be used up, nor shall the jar of oil run dry, until the day the* Lord *sends rain on the earth*" (1 Kings 17:14).

It is something to stay by a brook, as Elijah did, and be fed by ravens. I think that would take quite a bit of faith! But it is something else to have to believe God, not only for yourself, but also for a widow and her son, too. But Elijah knew the power of confession!

When you have victories, watch closely because the enemy wants to steal them from you. After the victory with the oil and meal, the widow's son died,

Two Confessions for a Balanced Identity

and she really had some deep questions about his death. She asked Elijah, *"What have I to do with you, O man of God? Have you come to me to bring my sin to remembrance, and to kill my son?"* (1 Kings 17:18).

Elijah took the woman's son in his arms and carried the body into another room. He prayed, "God, what has happened?" God was leading Elijah step-by-step into a deeper commitment of faith. First, he had to believe for his own life. Then he had to believe for two more lives to be sustained. But now, he had to believe for the restoration of a life!

He prayed, "Let this child's soul come into him again." God was bringing Elijah into faith for resurrection! The child's soul came into him again, and he lived. The woman was so deeply touched by the miracle that she told Elijah, *"I know that you are a man of God, and that the word of the LORD in your mouth is the truth"* (1 Kings 17:24).

The next step God was preparing Elijah for would be the biggest moment yet! After several years of drought, God said to Elijah, *"Go, present yourself to Ahab, and I will send rain on the earth"* (1 Kings 18:1).

Elijah met with Ahab and said, "Call all the prophets of Baal and the people of Israel to Mt. Carmel.

Then let's each build an altar with a sacrifice. I will call on the name of the Lord to consume the sacrifice, and you call on your gods. The god who answers by fire will be God."

I thought, *You stupid nut, Ahab! Don't you remember that God talked to Moses from a burning bush? Don't you remember that God led the Israelites by fire at night in the wilderness?* You can go through the whole Bible and find that God is a God of fire. Many Scripture references in the Bible say that God is a consuming fire! (see Exodus 24:17; Deuteronomy 4:24; 9:3; and Hebrews 12:29.) He sent the Holy Ghost and fire, didn't He? Obviously, even though he was an Israelite, Ahab had no knowledge of the God of Israel.

The Bible didn't give any particular order for the way Baal's altar was constructed, because it wasn't important. But there is a specific description of how Elijah rebuilt Israel's altar because God always does things in divine order. I believe that the men of Israel came under deep conviction watching the altar being rebuilt. In their days of following Baal, the children of Israel had allowed their altar to fall into neglect. It was made from 12 stones, each one representing one of Israel's 12 tribes. Looking on, I think someone may

Two Confessions for a Balanced Identity

have said, "That rock stands for my tribe, the tribe of Asher. I let that rock fall from the altar, but Elijah is restoring it to its rightful place for me."

Elijah told the prophets of Baal, "You call on your god first; the god who answers by fire is God." The prophets prayed, they screamed, they cut themselves, they did all sorts of things. I can't help but laugh at the way Elijah handled the situation — he made fun of them! He said, "Maybe your god is on vacation. Maybe he just can't hear, or is taking a nap, or is deaf."

The sarcastic humor really spurred the false prophets on, but nothing happened. Finally, at the time of the evening sacrifice, Elijah stopped them and said, "Enough is enough. Now it's my turn."

Of all things, Elijah had them pour 12 waterpots of water over the sacrifice. It hadn't rained for over three years, so had we been there that day, we might have said, "Elijah, what a waste! What are you doing?" But, by faith, Elijah was saying, "Each tribe of Israel is going to experience revival!" After pouring the 12 pots of water on the sacrifice, Elijah prayed this simple prayer:

Rebuild: Restoring Your God-Given Identity

"Hear me, O LORD, hear me, that this people may know that You are the LORD God, and that You have turned their hearts back to You again." Then the fire of the LORD fell and consumed the burnt sacrifice, and the wood and the stones and the dust, and it licked up the water that was in the trench.
(1 KINGS 18:37-38)

Fire usually doesn't come down, does it? Fire usually goes up! But this was God's fire that consumed the sacrifice, the stones, the water — everything! God had accepted the sacrifice for the sins of Israel. *"When all the people saw it, they fell on their faces; and they said, "'The LORD, He is God! The LORD, He is God!'"* (1 Kings 18:39).

Here the people followed the sacrifice for their sin with a confession of God's power. Elijah told them, "Everyone who is for God, stand with me." The Israelites gathered around Elijah, and then he said, "Do you see those prophets of Baal? Kill them!" There were 450 false prophets, and all of them were killed that day by the men of Israel.

Two Confessions for a Balanced Identity

It was finally time for rain because the people had repented, stood up for their God, and killed the prophets of Baal. There had been repentance from sin, as well as confession of God's goodness.

Elijah sent Ahab away to get some food, then Elijah went to the top of the mountain and put his face between his knees to pray fervently. I believe he prayed, "God, we have met the conditions of your Word, and you said that rain would come." Elijah had a servant with him, whom he told to "Go look toward the sea for any clouds."

The servant looked, came back, and said, "No clouds." But, you see, the Bible tells us to hold fast to our professions of faith without wavering because God is faithful to His promises. Elijah sent the servant to look for a cloud seven times, and the seventh time the servant said, "I saw a cloud — not a very big one — the size of a man's hand."

Elijah said, "That's it! It is going to rain!" There were no storm clouds, yet Elijah confessed his faith with his mouth. Did he get what he said? Yes, he got it. You will find that through all of Elijah's life, he always confessed things before he saw them. If you see something, you are in the sense realm, not the faith realm. But Elijah was walking in faith, just as we are to walk: *"For we walk by faith, not by sight"* (2 Corinthians 5:7).

Then Elijah said, "Hurry up, Ahab, let's go before it rains! Ahab started off in a chariot toward Jezreel, when something wonderful happened to Elijah: *"Then the hand of the Lord came upon Elijah; and he girded up his loins and ran ahead of Ahab to the entrance of Jezreel"* (1 Kings 18:46).

The hands spoken of in this chapter really thrill me. Whenever you confess God's Word, I think you leave your handprint on heaven. I think that when Elijah's servant saw a cloud the size of a man's hand, God was saying, "Elijah, your faith has touched heaven." James 4:8 tells us, *"Draw near to God and He will draw near to you. Cleanse your hands, you sinners; and purify your hearts, you double-minded."* Whenever you draw close to God with your confession, which brings cleansing, He also draws close to you. When Jesus faced Pilate, Pilate washed his hands, declaring he was innocent of Jesus's blood (see Matthew 27:24). But that washing wasn't with repentance, which brings forgiveness.

Two Confessions for a Balanced Identity

In Elijah's case, he was touched by the hand of the Lord, and he ran down the mountain into the city under an anointing of supernatural strength. Elijah received what he said. A centurion once told Jesus, *"Say the Word, and my servant will be healed"* (Luke 7:7). That centurion also received what he said. The woman who was afflicted with an issue of blood also received what she confessed: *"If only I may touch His clothes, I shall be made well"* (Mark 5:28). She was made whole. Joshua told the sun and the moon to stand still, and they did.

Stabilizing Your Identity

We must watch our confessions. I think that sometimes we need to look in the mirror and say, "God, this mouth has two purposes. It is for confessing sin — my sin, not everybody else's; and it is also for confessing your Word and its power."

Proverbs 12:14 says, *"A man will be satisfied with good by the fruit of his mouth."* God wants to satisfy you by the fruit of your mouth! Are you dissatisfied and discontent, but you don't know why? Perhaps you need to stop speaking words of discontentment.

God wants your thoughts and speech to line up with His Word. Philippians 4:8 is the key:

> *Finally, brethren, whatever things are true, whatever things are noble, whatever things are just, whatever things are pure, whatever things are lovely, whatever things are of good report, if there is any virtue and if there is anything praiseworthy — meditate on these things.*

You can stabilize your identity totally and overcome the enemy by being established in these two confessions: the confession of sin and the confession of faith. Psalm 17:4 says, *"Concerning the works of men, by the word of Your lips, I have kept away from the paths of the destroyer."*

The enemy wants to come in and pull down the walls and gates of your identity. But you can overcome the enemy of your identity through diligence in your confession. Give your identity a good report with the Word, and you will accelerate the Lord's work in conforming your identity to that of His Son's. Remember, it is God who works in you to will and to do his good pleasure (see Philippians 2:13).

Chapter Twelve

Our Identities Are Important to God

:::

His Vision for You

Have you ever felt as though you were just one in a crowd and God wasn't personally concerned about you? I think that all of us have felt like this, especially at times when the enemy was trying to get us into a negative frame of mind. Maybe these thoughts came when negative circumstances seemed overwhelming, or when we didn't feel good physically. Sometimes we feel this way when, after having prayed about something for years, we just get upset with the Lord and ask, "What? Don't you care?"

I want you to know that God is personally concerned about you, and you are not forgotten in a crowd. You can see this by looking at a woman who appeared to have been lost in a crowd, but she wasn't lost to Jesus. To God, we aren't lost at all. In fact, there could be a crowd of one million people, and if one of them had faith, God would see it. He sees faith and is attracted by faith.

The woman in the crowd had an issue of blood, and her story is told in three of the four gospels. Because of her infirmity, she was considered to be "unclean."

The woman had done every possible thing to obtain a cure, had spent every penny she owned, yet the issue of blood remained. As her story unfolds, you find that she was confessing something with her mouth that radically changed her identity, spirit, and physical body as no earthly physician could!

The woman heard that Jesus was passing through the streets of her town, and she heard that He had done many miracles for people. She thought, *I've got to get in on this.*

The woman rushed out to the street where Jesus was, and she probably fought her way past hundreds of people who were following Him that day. Then

Our Identities Are Important to God

she did something unusual. She did not come up and touch his shoulder or arm. She did not confront the Lord and ask Him for healing. Instead, she bent forward and reached out to touch the hem of the Lord's garment.

Why didn't the woman just come up right in front of Jesus? She couldn't do that because, by Levitical law, her unclean state prevented her from touching any man while she had an issue of blood. Anything she touched or sat upon had to be cleansed in a special way. Not only was the woman physically miserable, but her social and spiritual life suffered, too. She was cut off from worship because an unclean person could not enter the synagogue. She couldn't go anywhere with friends because she couldn't touch things. She had tried everything, and Jesus was her very last resort. How many times do we make Jesus our last resort? But last or not, He gave the woman what she needed. The scriptural accounts tell of the woman's healing in several different ways:

> *Now a woman, having a flow of blood for twelve years, who had spent all her livelihood on physicians and could not be healed by any,*

> *came from behind and touched the border of His garment. And immediately her flow of blood stopped.* (LUKE 8:43-44)

> *For she said, "If only I may touch His clothes, I shall be made well." Immediately the fountain of her blood was dried up, and she felt in her body that she was healed of the affliction.* (MARK 5:28-29)

I thought it was interesting that the fountain of blood, the source of the woman's issue of blood, was healed. Sometimes symptoms are taken care of through medication, but we don't cure the actual sickness. For instance, we may take something to ease the headache and sneezing of a cold but not actually be rid of the cold itself. But this woman knew in herself that she had been completely healed of the plague that she had suffered.

When the woman touched the hem of Jesus's garment, He stopped in His tracks, looked around, and said, "*Who touched Me?*"

Peter said, "That isn't a very sensible question. Here we are in a crowd of people where everyone

Our Identities Are Important to God

is touching you, and you ask, 'Who touched me?' Everyone is touching you!" Then Jesus said, *"Somebody touched Me, for I perceived power going out from Me"* (Luke 8:46).

You can't ever touch Jesus in faith without receiving the miracle power you need for your situation. The woman knew that she had no choice but to confess what had happened when the Lord asked, *"Who touched Me?"* She knew that, according to the Levitical law, she had been wrong to touch Jesus. Trembling, she stepped up in front of Him and declared before Him and all the people why she had touched Him and that she had been healed immediately.

I believe that Jesus called the woman apart from the crowd because He wanted her to confess her faith. In Matthew 10:32, Jesus said, *"Therefore whoever confesses Me before men, him I will also confess before My Father who is in heaven."* When the woman confessed her faith in front of the crowd, Jesus spoke tenderly, *"Daughter, be of good comfort: thy faith hath made thee whole; go in peace"* (Luke 8:48 KJV).

When the woman confessed her faith in the Lord, she received far more than healing. She was an outcast, an unclean woman, yet Jesus called her "daughter." Then He said, "*Be of good comfort.*" The word "comfort" is a really great word. In the Greek, it means "to be of good courage, . . . to be confident, hopeful." The woman came to him trembling with fear, but he gave her a new identity of courage, boldness, and confidence.

Then the Lord told the woman, "*Thy faith hath made thee whole.*" The Greek word for "whole" here is "*sōzō.*" *Sōzō* means "to save, keep safe and sound, to rescue from danger or destruction." This Greek word speaks not just to someone's physical body but also to their spiritual condition. A person who is not a Christian may have a healthy physical body, but if he is still incomplete in his spirit, he is not whole. But this woman was made complete in her body, her mind, and her spirit.

Not only did Jesus save the woman, give her a new identity, and call her "daughter" for her confession of faith, but He also said, "*Go in peace.*" She had taken a risk in standing before hundreds of people to tell the Lord what she had done. Now she could go in a spirit of peace. What a transformation this woman received!

After reading the story of this woman's healing, I could not help but wonder why she reached down to touch the hem of the Lord's garment. Why not brush by his shoulder? Wouldn't that be as effective? I found my answer in Numbers 15:

> *Again the* LORD *spoke to Moses, saying, "Speak to the children of Israel: Tell them to make tassels on the corners of their garments throughout their generations, and to put a blue thread in the tassels of the corners. And you shall have the tassel, that you may look upon it and remember all the commandments of the* LORD *and do them . . ."*
> (NUMBERS 15:37-39)

God said, "I want all of the sons of Israel to have a fringe on their garments to remind them of My commandments. This fringe will remind them of My presence." By seeing the fringes on their garments, the men of Israel would be reminded that God was their Lord, and they were not to be involved with idols.

Blue has always signified the healing power of God and represents the Word of God, so in a way, the thread of blue underneath the fringe represented the presence of God. That little thread of blue was saying, "Wherever I go, the Word of God goes with me. I want to go God's way." Jewish men would wear prayer shawls, or Tallits, with those tassels on the corners. In Hebrew, the corner is called the wing, or *kanaph,* and represents the authority of the one who is wearing it. So that day, she touched the symbol of Jesus's authority and found healing in His wings.

The woman with the issue of blood had reached through the crowd to touch the presence of God! Even though she had been just one in a crowd, her faith had set her apart. When Jesus called her before Him, she was face-to-face with the Son of God. I'm sure that, to her, it didn't appear that there was anyone else present besides her and Jesus. God loves every one of us just as though there were only one to love.

I especially like the account of the woman's healing in Matthew, which tells us that when the woman heard about Jesus, *"She said to herself, 'If only I may touch His garment, I shall be made well'"* (9:21). The woman received exactly what she said: wholeness in her spirit, soul, and body. Apparently, she had tried many cures for her issue of blood, but none of them had worked. Yet because of her words, the source of her issue of blood dried up when she touched the Lord's garment. Jesus did not say, *"My* faith healed you." He said, *"Your* faith healed you." Philemon 1:6 tells you how faith is released: *"The sharing of your faith may become effective by the acknowledgment of every good thing which is in you in Christ Jesus."*

How do you turn your faith loose? The woman made her faith effectual, or "energetic," by her confession of faith, by speaking it with her mouth: "If I touch the hem of His garment, I shall be whole." Why? Because she knew that she was touching the Word of God and the healing power of God.

There is a beautiful psalm about how good and pleasant it is for brethren to dwell together in unity. It is Psalm 133:2 that says of the anointing:

It is like the precious oil upon the head,
Running down on the beard,
The beard of Aaron,
Running down on the edge of his garments.

The priestly anointing of Aaron started at the top of his head and flowed down past the skirts of his garment to his feet. Aaron was a high priest, but Jesus is *the* High Priest, whose garment you can touch by faith today.

Do you need an anointing of healing in your identity? Perhaps you have struggled with a bad temper. Maybe you have just been living in defeat. Whatever the problem, Jesus wants to change your life through the words you speak. By speaking words of faith, you are reaching out and touching the presence of God. You aren't just another person in the crowd. Your faith will set you apart. That's the key to your entire identity transformation: turn your faith loose! You turn your faith loose by turning your mouth loose — and by doing so, you loose wholeness for your identity, spirit, and life.

Our Identities Are Important to God

God's Vision for Others

Since God is personally concerned about our individual identities, it is important that we, in turn, are concerned with the identities of others. God doesn't save us so that we can sit around and do nothing. He saves us so that we can share what we have with the rest of the world.

In the New Testament, a man named Barnabas gave us a beautiful example of how we can, by faith, get God's vision of transformation for others as well as ourselves. According to Acts 4:36, Barnabas's name means "son of encouragement" and he was a Levite from the little island of Cyprus. Evidently, he was very wealthy, for the Bible speaks of how he came to the apostles and, having sold some land, brought the money, and laid it at their feet in his commitment to the ministry. He was very excited about the gospel and the idea of seeing the body of Christ brought to the uttermost parts of the earth.

One day, Barnabas heard about a man who was preaching the gospel. Everyone was afraid to talk to the man because, in the past, he had been guilty of persecuting and killing many Christians. In fact, he had consented to the death of Stephen, one of the church's primary deacons. The disciples of Jesus thought, *This is a trap. He wants to get our names so that he can have us killed.*

> *But Barnabas took him and brought him to the apostles. And he declared to them how he had seen the Lord on the road, and that He had spoken to him, and how he had preached boldly at Damascus in the name of Jesus.*
>
> (ACTS 9:27)

The man whom Barnabas brought to the apostles was named Saul. He was a devoted Pharisee who had studied the Scriptures at the feet of Gamaliel, one of the day's most learned Jews. Saul would become Paul, the apostle who would write more than half of the New Testament — a paradox to both Jews and Christians alike.

Barnabas was concerned that the body of Christ grow in the knowledge of their Lord and fully understand their new identities as Christians. He wasn't content with just seeing people converted, but was interested in their spiritual growth afterward.

Our Identities Are Important to God

Whenever you read about Barnabas, he was making good confessions about others. It's one thing to make a good confession for yourself, the woman with the issue of blood confessed that the Lord could make her whole. But we can get so hung up on ourselves that we forget how God wants to use us in the identities of other people. We need to make good confessions for them too.

The next positive confession made by Barnabas is found in Acts chapter 11. A tremendous revival broke out among the gentiles, and Barnabas' first reaction was, "These people need to hear from Saul!"

Then Barnabas departed for Tarsus to seek Saul. And when he had found him, he brought him to Antioch. So it was that for a whole year they assembled with the church and taught a great many people. And the disciples were first called Christians in Antioch. (ACTS 11:25-26)

Barnabas thought, *Saul has been educated by the best teachers, so he fully understands the meaning of the gospel. He knows the Word well, and he has had a personal encounter with Jesus Christ.* Barnabas brought Saul to the gentiles as a teacher. While Saul was teaching, God used the time as a training period before launching him into full-time ministry abroad.

God uses everything possible in your life to prepare you for your next step. God's divine goal for Christians is that they be conformed to the image of Christ Jesus. But there is also a plan for your individual life. God wants to prepare you to fulfill that plan. He definitely used Saul's time in Antioch as preparation for what would be his first missionary journey.

Eventually, Barnabas and Saul took a young, on-fire convert named John Mark under their wing, to train him in the ministry. Shortly afterward, Barnabas and Saul were set apart for their ministries of evangelism:

> *As they* [leaders of the church at Antioch] *ministered to the Lord and fasted, the Holy Spirit said, "Now separate to Me Barnabas and Saul for the work to which I have called them." Then, having fasted and prayed, and laid hands on them, they sent them away.*
> (ACTS 13:2-3)

Our Identities Are Important to God

Those ministering and fasting with Saul and Barnabas laid hands on them and sent them forth to preach. From that time on, Saul was called Paul. Nothing in the Scriptures is an accident, of course, so why the name change? Later on, you see that Paul had a definite call to preach to the gentiles. His Jewish name had been Saul, but now he needed a gentile name: Paul.

Paul and Barnabas started out on their journey, and they brought John Mark, Barnabas's cousin, with them. Some really tremendous things happened, but one of the low points of the mission was when John Mark became very homesick and had to return to Antioch. Apparently, this really upset Paul. Nonetheless, there were many miracles on this first missionary journey.

When Barnabas and Paul returned to Antioch, the people were thrilled to hear about the wonderful things that had happened to the men. Not long afterward, they decided to return to the cities where men had received the Lord. Barnabas told Paul, "Let's give John Mark a second chance."

Paul said, "No, I wouldn't think of taking him. He's just a mama's boy. He had to go home before we completed the first missionary journey, and he'll probably do it again."

I love what Acts 15:37 says: "*Barnabas was determined to take with them John called Mark.*" Barnabas was determined that this young convert's ministry would be developed. His confession about other identities is so positive!

Barnabas's insistence that John Mark go on the mission just made Paul angrier, and there were very sharp words between him and Barnabas. Finally, they agreed to go on separate journeys: Paul would go with Silas, and Barnabas would take John Mark.

It seems such a shame that Paul and Barnabas had a disagreement, but the story still has a happy ending. Mark, under Barnabas's instruction, began to develop in ministry. He may have been a baby on the first journey, but he grew up.

After the missionary journey, Mark became such an ardent follower of Jesus that the apostle Peter became his tutor. Peter loved Mark so much that later Peter called him "my son." Mark, being like Peter's son, heard the instructor's every word about Jesus. Mark soaked in one firsthand account after another.

Then God began to speak to Mark about writing a Gospel.

Mark could have said, "I'm not worthy. I was never an original apostle." But I believe God said, "You were taught by an original apostle, and I want you to write his words down."

Today, the Gospel of Mark that is in our Bibles was written by the Mark about whom Paul said, "No way. He'll never amount to anything." Mark might have just given up on the ministry because he had been turned down by those more seasoned in the ministry than he was. But Barnabas saw beyond appearances and received a vision of faith for the young man.

This story ends so beautifully with Mark ultimately being accepted by Paul. To the Colossians, Paul wrote, "Welcome Mark if he comes to you" (4:10), and then in 2 Timothy 4:11 Paul said, *"Get Mark and bring him with you, for he is useful to me for ministry."* What a compliment to Mark! Not only did Paul say, "He is a good minister," but also, "I need him here." Mark, the deserter, became Mark, the minister and writer of the gospel.

Did Barnabas and Paul ever make up? Yes, because Paul wrote about Barnabas in 1 Corinthians 9:6, which was written about 55 AD, before the book of Acts was written, most likely close to 65 AD. Maybe Paul told Barnabas, "I'm going to have to learn to like meat, because I have to eat crow. I never thought that Mark would work out, and you showed me differently. Your positive confession made him profitable in the ministry."

I want you to know that God has sent you to have more than just an identity change in your own life. He wants you to help others have changes of identity in their lives. God wants you ministering to others with honest words of faith. He wants you to use positive words to build character and mold their identities.

How did Barnabas know that "Saul" would become "Paul" and that Mark would become a mighty minister of Christ? He knew because he looked beyond God's concern for his own identity and loved others deeply enough to extend that same concern to them. After all, the beauty of an identity that is complete in Jesus Christ is that it reaches out to help transform the identities of others.

Chapter Thirteen

A New You

:::

As stated at the beginning of this book, our goal is to get the walls of our identities rebuilt so that we can be fit temples in which God can dwell. But the devil has been stealing our identities ever since the fall of Adam and Eve. The truth is that we are made in the image of God and, as such, have a specific, God-given purpose and identity — to be conformed to that image, which Satan hates.

As we have seen, our spirits, souls, and bodies can be totally and radically transformed to match the identities God has for us — unique and distinctively different from that of others — by the power of the Holy Spirit and the renewing of our minds through the Word. We can apply its truths to every facet of our lives to take back what the devil has stolen and rebuild the walls and gates of our identities, thereby confirming who we are in Christ.

The book of Nehemiah provides us with not only a look at the history of Israel's return from exile but also a look at how the returning exiles shed the identities they had acquired in exile. In so doing, they rebuilt their identities according to what God declared for them. Nehemiah is a beautiful typology of how to rebuild damaged and broken areas of our identities to become a temple fit for God to dwell in.

Celebrate!

The wall surrounding Jerusalem, which symbolizes security and protection, was completed and the gates rehung in just 52 days. What a day of rejoicing that must have been! They had survived numerous threats from their enemies, developed strategies, and worked together to accomplish their goal. They were beginning to form their new identities, and in so doing, a dominated people were gaining dominion over their own identities because they trusted in their God. In addition, those who had tried to thwart the rebuilding were taught a mighty lesson:

> *So the wall was finished on the twenty-fifth day of Elul, in fifty-two days. And it happened, when all our enemies heard of it, and all the nations around us saw these things, that they were very disheartened in their own eyes; for they perceived that this work was done by our God.* (NEHEMIAH 6:15-16)

Throughout the rebuilding of the walls and rehanging of the gates, we see God's sovereign plan being worked out; it is evident that He is truly involved in the lives of His people and orchestrates history to carry out His sovereign plans — and even Israel's enemies realized it!

That includes His plans for rebuilding your identity. Your past can become the building blocks for your new identity; masterfully orchestrated by the Holy Spirit to accomplish His goals for your life. Your past is turned around and is now under the blood of Christ. You are a new creation because of

Jesus's sacrifice. And the Holy Spirit is directing the rebuilding project.

This is beautifully illustrated in Nehemiah. Those who had gone into exile had suddenly realized their great loss. The Israelites had thought their nation would exist forever; it was secure because the temple of God, and thus God's presence, were there. But they had not only lost their individual identities, but they had lost their national identity as well. As we have already seen, instead of "Israelites," the exiles referred to themselves as servants (see Nehemiah 9:36).

I believe that Ezra and Nehemiah realized this because, following the completion of the wall, they called the people to celebrate the Feast of Tabernacles, a reminder of how God had spared their ancestors from death and delivered them from slavery in Egypt. Nehemiah 8 and 9 record that they called an assembly of the "children of Israel" so that they could finally discard these old identities. The people came together, *"fasting, in sackcloth, and with dust on their heads"* and *"separated themselves from all foreigners"* (see Nehemiah 9:1-2).

Ezra read from the Book of the Law of the Lord (the Word) for about three hours, followed by another three hours spent worshiping the Lord their God and confessing their faults and sins, including those of their ancestors. The people were cut to the quick as they were instructed in what God required of them. They began to weep and mourn over their failures, but Nehemiah and Ezra built them up instead of disciplining them. They basically told them to celebrate:

> *"This day is holy to the LORD your God; do not mourn nor weep." For all the people wept, when they heard the words of the Law. Then he said to them, "Go your way, eat the fat, drink the sweet, and send portions to those for whom nothing is prepared; for this day is holy to our Lord. Do not sorrow, for the joy of the LORD is your strength."* (NEHEMIAH 8:9-10)

By reading the Law, Ezra had reminded them of their history as a people, giving them a foundation on which to stand and proclaim God's covenant promises. They were reminded that God is a good God and that their own strength was found in the joy of their Lord. And the people celebrated with great joy because they finally understood the words that had been read to them! Then, to fulfill what they now understood, they gladly celebrated the Feast of Tabernacles (or Feast of Booths), a post-exilic declaration of their own exodus:

> *So the whole assembly of those who had returned from the captivity made booths and sat under the booths; for since the days of Joshua the son of Nun until that day the children of Israel had not done so. And there was very great gladness.* (NEHEMIAH 8:17)

Little by little, as the Word was getting into them, they were beginning to realize their own new identities as servants of the Most-High God, instead of servants and slaves of a foreign king. They could finally rejoice and be glad of who they were spiritually, a group of individuals who had worked together in unity to build a wall of security in the historic capital of their former nation. In doing so, they trusted God to revive them individually and redeem them as a people.

Is it any wonder that, as a result of their efforts over 52 days and the celebrations that followed, the people agreed to a whole new series of reforms designed to mold them into God's people? After Ezra's fast and long prayer of confession in chapters eight and nine of Nehemiah, the people decided to reaffirm their covenant with God. They agreed to keep the law and the Sabbath, pay tithes, and observe strict marriage laws. Nehemiah's new religious and social reforms affected many who had intermarried, including priests and Levites. And all the people agreed that they would put away the foreigners from among them.

God had remained faithful to His ancient covenant with His people. Their identity was no longer centered on the existence of their political nation. Their new identity now centered on the Law and the rebuilt temple, where they could go to commune with God who would guide them individually and corporately to fulfill His plans for their lives. Finally, the emphasis was now on their identity as the people of God — God's original plan for them.

Your New Kingdom Identity

This new identity of the exiles foreshadows that of our own identities as Christians. When you accepted Jesus as your Savior, the old man passed away. Even if you have a past that you aren't proud of, He can use your past experiences and failures to mold and shape you into the person He made you to be.

When you became a new creation, you also became a part of a kingdom of priests and kings that knows no political boundaries (see Revelation 1:6). Your new identity is a spiritual identity, one that is orchestrated by a loving Father, initiated by the King of Kings, and directed by the Holy Spirit. You may be a member of a specific congregation, but more importantly, you are a member of *the* Church, the body of Christ, which includes peoples from all nations, tribes, and tongues, and supersedes all political boundaries.

The covenant of the Old Testament foreshadows many of God's provisions for you today. The promises of the new covenant guarantee you, as a citizen of the kingdom of God, certain rights and freedoms. As a believer, you are righteous: *"But of Him you are* in Christ Jesus, who became for us wisdom from God — and righteousness and sanctification and redemption" (1 Corinthians 1:30). Regardless of your past, you are forgiven and have the promise of eternal life. Furthermore, righteousness makes you fearless in Satan's presence.

One of the most precious blessings is that you are united with God through the blood of Christ; you can produce the same fruit that He does, and you have the same life as Jesus because your life comes from Him. His bloodline is now your bloodline. Your new identity is that of royalty through the King of Kings.

Those in covenant with God also have a revelation of God. This revelation comes through studying the life of Jesus and through the Holy Spirit. The returning exiles, who both repented and wept over their past, became more aware of who God is and what He desired to do for them through studying the Word. Just like them, you can know His works and His ways, but most importantly you can know Him. Jesus tells you everything He learns from the Father, giving you a revelation of God. You can become so intimately acquainted with Him that you are also called His "friend": *"No longer do I call you servants, for a servant does not know what his master is doing; but I have called you friends, for all things that I heard from My Father I have made known to you"* (John 15:15). Like the returning exiles, you needn't think of yourself as a servant or a slave to sin. Your new identity means you are a friend of God, freed from the bondages of the past.

Also, like the returning exiles, you are blessed with victory over your enemies. Jesus's supremacy over everything means that He has disarmed every power and authority that comes against you — He triumphed over them on the cross. Your enemies were defeated almost 2,000 years ago — fear, discouragement, self-doubt, generational curses — have all been conquered on the cross because Jesus:

> *... having wiped out the handwriting of requirements that was against us, which was contrary to us. And He has taken it out of the way, having nailed it to the cross. Having disarmed principalities and powers, He made a public spectacle of them, triumphing over them in it.* (COLOSSIANS 2:14-15)

Nehemiah and the Israelites gained victory over their enemies through the power of prayer. They met each threat with prayer. Prayer is your hotline to God. It's instant — two-way and faster than the blink of an eye. God hears you: *"Thus says the Lord . . . 'Call to Me, and I will answer you, and show you great and mighty things, which you do not know' "* (Jeremiah 33:2–3). You must maintain communication with God. Keep a clear conscience and live obediently to the Word. When you sin, receive forgiveness through confession and remain clean of sin. Never forget, the devil can use sin in your life to take your confidence away.

The Israelites gained authority over their enemies, who I believe were sent by Satan to thwart Nehemiah's assignment to rebuild the wall. According to Luke 10:19, as a Christian, you have power and authority over the power of Satan and his demons. Your might and strength have nothing to do with your size, poise, training, or physical strength. Not only is the joy of the Lord your strength, but your victory comes from the authority you were given and the power you possess through Jesus.

Part of that power and authority comes because you have the name of Jesus. When the returning

Israelites encountered obstacles from the local people who complained to King Darius, the Jews asked Darius to investigate the historical records in which Cyrus had given them the blessing and authority to rebuild. They used the authority and name of a governing monarch to put an end to the opposition. Likewise, the name of Jesus always bears fruit, for it is the name above all names. In the name of Jesus, you can do all things. John 16:23–24 tells us that the Father will give you whatever you ask when you use the name of Jesus. So, whatever needs you have, claim them in the name of Jesus and put the devil to flight.

From the moment you accept Jesus Christ as your Savior and Lord, the power of the new covenant is yours. You can now walk in victory every day of your life because of who you are in Christ. You have the authority, Word, blood, and the name of Jesus Christ to wield as your weapons against the enemy. In other words, your new identity is firmly established in your relationship with Christ. You can now become the mighty man or woman of God He made you to be.

End Notes

Chapter One

3. *49,000 Israelites returned* . . . : LaSort, William Sanford, David Allan Hubbard, Frederic William Bush. *Old Testament Survey, The Message, Form, and Background of the Old Testament*, 2nd ed. (Grand Rapids: William B. Eerdmans Publishing Company, 1996), 53.

5. *Nehemiah's name is "consolation of Jehovah"* . . . : James Strong, *The New Strong's Complete Dictionary of Bible Words* (Nashville: Thomas Nelson Publishers, 1996), s.v. "Nehemiah."

5. *Paraklēsis*

7. *The Hebrew word for "redeemed" means* . . . : Merriam-Webster, s.v. "Redeem." https://www.merriam-webster.com/dictionary/redeem.

9. *One of the meanings of "Sanballat" is "enemy in secret."* . . . : Bible Study Tools, s.v. "Sanballat." https://www.biblestudytools.com/dictionaries/hitchcocks-bible-names/sanballat.html.

25. *Valley of Hinnom which is analogous of hell* . . . : Bible Study Tools, s.v. "Hinnom." https://www.biblestudytools.com/dictionary/hinnom/.

Chapter Two

31. *Nehemiah tells of 12 gates* . . . : Julie Almanrode. "The Gates and Walls of Nehemiah." Posted October 7, 2016. *Tent Stake Ministries.* http://tentstakeministries.net/2016/10/the-gates-and-walls-of-nehemiah/.

Rebuild: Restoring Your God-Given Identity

34. *Eliashib* . . . *His name means "God will restore"*: James Strong, *The New Strong's Complete Dictionary of Bible Words*, s.v. "Eliashib."

34. *Energēs* . . . James Strong. *Strong's Exhaustive Concordance Complete and Unabridged.* (Grand Rapids: Baker Book House, 1980), "Energēs."

35. *The Hebrew word for "fish" means "squirming"*: James Strong, *The New Strong's Complete Dictionary of Bible Words*, s.v. "Dâ'g."

40. *Hivite means "snake"*: *Religion Wiki*, s.v. "Hivite." https://religion.wikia.org/wiki/Hivite#:~:text=According%20to%20traditional%20Hebrew%20sources,snakes%20looking%20for%20fertile%20land

43. *Nethinim, which means "ones given to duty"*: James Strong, *The New Strong's Complete Dictionary of Bible Words*, s.v. "Nethinim."

45. *Valley are sometimes used figuratively . . .* : W. E. Vine, *Vine's Complete Expository Dictionary of Old and New Testament Words* (Nashville: Nelson, 1997), s.v. "Valley."

Chapter Three

64. *Miphkad means "assignment"*: James Strong, *The New Strong's Complete Dictionary of Bible Words*, s.v. "Miphkad."

73. *The Ephraim Gate is the "double fruit" gate*: James Strong, *The New Strong's Complete Dictionary of Bible Words*, s.v. "Ephraim."

Chapter Four

90. *Admonish means . . .* : W. E. Vine, *Vine's Complete Expository Dictionary of Old and New Testament Words* (Nashville: Nelson, 1997), s.v. "Admonition, Admonish." See "nouthesia"/ "noutheteó."

90. *I like this definition: "[Admonishment] . . .":* Bible Hub, "3560.noutheteó." https://biblehub.com/greek/3560.htm.

Chapter Five

99. *Gideon had everything going for him. His name means "feller" or "great warrior,"* . . . : Strong, *The New Strong's Complete Dictionary of Bible Words*, s.v. "Gidʻôwn."

104. *Gideon saw God revealed as Jehovah Shalom*: *Bible Study Tools*, s.v. "Jehovah-shalom." https://www.biblestudytools.com/dictionary/jehovah-shalom/.

107. *Gideon is called "Jerubbasheth," which means "shame will contend"* . . . : James Strong, *The New Strong's Complete Dictionary of Bible Words*, s.v. "Yᵉrubbesheth."

End Notes

107. *Gideon was clothed from his head to his toes in the Spirit of God*: Jay P. Green, Sr., *The Interlinear Bible* (Peabody: Hendrickson Publishers, 1984), 218.

Chapter Six

119. *Ahithophel's name means "brother of folly,"* . . . : James Strong, *The New Strong's Complete Dictionary of Bible Words*, s.v. "Ahithophel."

Chapter Seven

135. *Samson means "sunlight,"* . . . : James Strong, *The New Strong's Complete Dictionary of Bible Words*, s.v. "Samson."

135. *The Spirit of the Lord "rushed upon Samson and made him successful"* . . . : *Blue Letter Bible*, s.v. "Tsaw-lakh" https://www.blueletterbible.org/lexicon/h6743/kjv/wlc/0-1/

143. *Delilah, and her name means "feeble, delicate"*: James Strong, *The New Strong's Complete Dictionary of Bible Words*, s.v. "Delilah."

145. *To repent means to "turn back,"* . . . : James Strong, *The New Strong's Complete Dictionary of Bible Words*, s.v. "Repent."

146. *God's name, Adonai, which means "Master"*: Abarim Publications, "Adonai Meaning." https://www.abarim-publications.com/Meaning/Adonai.html#.X3YPyhSSm7o.

146. *Then in that same statement he used the word Yahweh,* . . . : James Strong, *The New Strong's Expanded Dictionary of Bible Words*, (Nashville: Thomas Nelson Publishers, 2001), s.v. "Yᵉhôvâh."

146. *Elohim. The Lord God. He is the "supreme God"* . . . : James Strong, *The New Strong's Complete Dictionary of Bible Words*, s.v. " 'Elōhîym."

146. *Elohim . . . our "creator," and the "mighty one."*: Abarim Publications, "Elohim Meaning." https://www.abarim-publications.com/Meaning/Elohim.html#.X3ZUlmhKiUk.

Chapter Nine

171. *Agape is the kind of love with which God loves us*: W. E. Vine, *Vine's Complete Expository Dictionary of Old and New Testament Words* (Nashville: Nelson, 1997), s.v. "Love."

171. *There the word love is "phileō,"* . . . : James Strong, *The New Strong's Expanded Dictionary of Bible Words*, s.v. "Philéō."

178. *Dunamis, or "miracle-working power"*: James Strong, *The New Strong's Expanded Dictionary of Bible Words*, s.v. "Dunamis."

Rebuild: Restoring Your God-Given Identity

Chapter Ten

179. *Because the child's name means "laughter"*: James Strong, *The New Strong's Expanded Dictionary of Bible Words*, s.v. "Isaac."

180. *"Eli" means "lofty"*. . . . : James Strong, *The New Strong's Expanded Dictionary of Bible Words*, s.v. "Eli."

180. *Hophni means "a pair of fists,"*. . . : James Strong, *The New Strong's Expanded Dictionary of Bible Words*, s.v. "Hophni."

180. *Phinehas means "mouth of a serpent"*. . . : James Strong, *The New Strong's Expanded Dictionary of Bible Words*, s.v. "Phinehas."

183. *"Samuel," meaning "heard of God"*: James Strong, *The New Strong's Expanded Dictionary of Bible Words*, s.v. "Samuel."

Chapter Eleven

194. *The Hebrew for "hidden part" is ṭuḥâ*. . . : James Strong, *Strong's Exhaustive Concordance Complete and Unabridged*, s.v. "ṭuḥâ."

201. *Elijah . . . means "Yahweh is my God,"* . . . *Brittanica*. s.v. "Elijah." https://www.britannica.com/biography/Elijah-Hebrew-prophet.

Chapter Twelve

218. *The word "comfort" . . . means . . .* : Bill Mounce. *BillMounce.com*, s.v. "Tharséō." https://www.billmounce.com/greek-dictionary/tharseo.

218. *The Greek word for "whole" . . .* : Bible Study Tools, s.v. "Sōzō." https://www.biblestudytools.com/lexicons/greek/nas/sozo.html.

220. *Blue has always signified the healing power of God . . .* : Jacob Olesen, "Biblical Meaning of Colors." https://www.color-meanings.com/biblical-meaning-colors/.

220. *In Hebrew, the corner is called the wing or kanaph and represents . . .* : BibleHub, s.v. "kanaph." https://biblehub.com/hebrew/3671.htm.

Receive Jesus Christ as Lord and Savior of Your Life

:::

You can have Jesus's joy, peace, protection, and provision in your life starting today. You can also know for sure that you will have life after death in heaven. God sent Jesus Christ to be the Savior of the world. First Timothy 2:5–6 says, *"For there is one God and one Mediator between God and men, the Man Christ Jesus, who gave Himself a ransom for all . . ."*

The Bible tells us how we can receive Jesus as Savior:

> *If you confess with your mouth the Lord Jesus and believe in your heart that God has raised Him from the dead, you will be*

saved. For with the heart one believes unto righteousness, and with the mouth confession is made unto salvation. (ROMANS 10:9-10)

Would you like to begin a personal relationship with God and Jesus right now? You can! Simply pray this prayer in sincerity:

Heavenly Father, I acknowledge that I need your help. I am not able to change my life or circumstances through my own efforts. I know that I have made some wrong decisions in my life, and at this moment I turn away from those ways of thinking and acting. I believe you have provided a way for me through Jesus to receive your blessings and help in my life. Right now, I believe and confess Jesus as my Lord and Savior. I ask Jesus to come into my heart and give me a new life, by your Spirit. I thank you for saving me and I ask for your grace and mercy in my life. I pray this in Jesus's name. Amen.

Receive Jesus Christ as Lord and Savior of Your Life

⁝⁝

If you just prayed to make Jesus your Lord, we want to know! Please call us today — toll free — at 888-637-4545.

We will pray for you and send you a special gift to help you in your new life with Christ.

About Marilyn Hickey

:::

Encouraging, optimistic, always upbeat and energetic, even in her later years, Marilyn Hickey actively ministers internationally. As founder and president of *Marilyn Hickey Ministries*, a non-profit ministry and humanitarian organization based in Denver, Colorado, Marilyn has impacted many countries worldwide; from disaster relief efforts in Haiti, Indonesia, and Pakistan to providing food for the hungry in Mexico, Costa Rica, Russia, and the Philippines. Her legacy includes significant ministry in Islamic countries. In 2016, over one million people attended her healing meeting in Karachi, Pakistan.

Marilyn has traveled to over 140 countries, and has held audiences with government leaders and heads of state all over the world. She was the first woman to join the board of directors for Dr. David Yonggi Cho (founder of the world's largest congregation, Yoido Full Gospel Church in South Korea). Along with her daughter, pastor Sarah Bowling, she co-hosts the daily television program, *Today with Marilyn & Sarah*, which is broadcast globally. *Today with Marilyn & Sarah* is shown in 130 countries with a potential viewing audience of over 2 billion households worldwide. Marilyn has also authored over 100 publications.

She and her late husband, Wallace, were married over 50 years and have two children and five grandchildren. Marilyn holds a Bachelor of Arts in Collective Foreign Languages from the University of Northern Colorado and an Honorary Doctor of Divinity from Oral Roberts University.

In 2015, Marilyn was honored at Oral Roberts University with the prestigious Lifetime Global Achievement Award. This award recognizes individuals, or organizations, that have made a significant impact in the history of ORU and around the world. In 2019, Marilyn also received an International

About Marilyn Hickey

Lifetime Peace Award from the Grand Imam and President of Pakistan.

In 2021, Marilyn was honored with two awards from the Assemblies of God Theological Seminary: The Pillar of Faith Award in acknowledgment of her worldwide impact on the church through biblical teaching and sustainable healing ministry; and the Smith Wigglesworth Award, given on behalf of the entire Assemblies of God fellowship in acknowledgment of her decades of service worldwide.

Marilyn's greatest passion and desire is to continue being a bridge-builder in countries around the world, and she shows no signs of stopping.

To learn more about Marilyn Hickey Ministries, visit:

:::

Marilyn Hickey Ministries: marilynandsarah.org
Check out our free downloads that include Bible reading plans, teaching notes, inspirational graphics, spiritual self-assessments, and lists of verses based on topic.

Online Master Classes: mentoredbymarilyn.org
Marilyn is passing her mantle on to you! Through her anointed master classes, you will be mentored in strategic areas that will take you to the next level of victory and fulfillment in your life and ministry. This is an incredible opportunity to mentored by Marilyn!

Connect with Marilyn:

- MarilynHickeyMinistries
- MarilynandSarah
- MarilynHickeyMinistries
- MarilynHickeyMinistries